DIVINE
INTERVENTION

Walnut Springs Press, LLC
110 South 800 West
Brigham City, Utah 84302
http://walnutspringspress.blogspot.com

ISBN: 978-1-935217-85-5

DIVINE
INTERVENTION
A STORY OF FAITH AND MIRACLES

Helen and Randy Hall

To all those who keep their faith despite adversity.

ACKNOWLEDGEMENTS

We would like to acknowledge the people who helped this book become a reality. First we would like to thank our children, whom we live for, as well as our relatives, friends, neighbors, and those people who attended our firesides and encouraged us to write a book about our experiences. We would also like to thank our beautiful niece, Julie Ransom, who teaches English and writing at BYU and helped us with the initial editing. Thanks to Susan Farrell for her constructive contribution. We would like to express our heartfelt appreciation to Sharon Reeder at Brigham Distributing, who brought us to the good people at Walnut Springs Press to bring this book to fruition. We owe a debt of gratitude to and loved working with Linda Mulleneaux, Amy Orton, and Garry Mitchell.

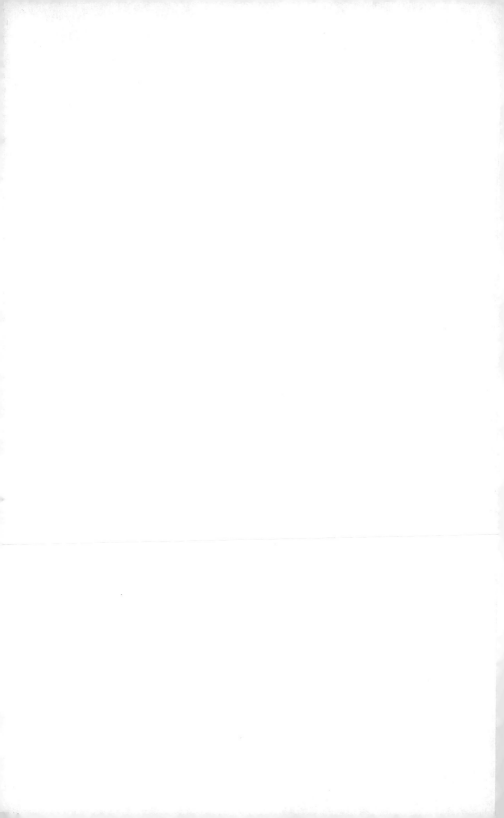

INTRODUCTION

HELEN

The first week of May 1994, I came home from running errands and found a message in my eleven-year-old daughter's handwriting, telling me to call Oprah Winfrey at the given number. "Yeah, right!" I laughed and did a quick mental scan of our friends and neighbors creative enough to come up with this prank. It was too late for April Fool's, but that had never stopped them before. Our friends had a history of pulling off some pretty fun-loving jokes on each other, from listing one neighbor's priceless antique gun collection for sale for $200 in the local want ads, to issuing official-looking cease and desist notices. So I could play along with this prank. As I dialed the number, trying to control my laughter, I wondered whom we knew with a co-conspirator in the 307 area code.

A very professional voice answered the phone with, "*Oprah Winfrey Show*, how can I help you?" I was sure she had checked her caller ID and was thinking, "Okay, this is the sucker that thinks she's calling Oprah Winfrey."

So, in a voice oozing with sarcasm, I said, "Soooo, is Oprah there?"

The lady politely replied, "She's not available right now. I'm Judy Banks, one of her writers. May I help you?"

I was thinking, *Oh, you are good, REAL good! But I'm not going to be fooled by you.*

I said in a mocking voice, "So, Judy is it? Well, Judy, how's it going? This is Helen Hall. I understand you called. I guess since I'm so famous and all, Oprah wants me to be on her show. Right?"

"Oprah is doing a show on intuition," she answered politely. "We picked up your story from the A.P. wire about some premonitions you had, and we thought it would be an interesting addition to the show."

The list of who could pull off this inspired prank was narrowing. For just a split, insane second I was about to say, "Is this really someone from the Oprah show?" However, the humbling thought of "Judy" busting up laughing and gleefully shouting, "A-ha! Gotcha!" kept me from folding. Instead, I continued to play along and said, "So Judy, tell me who you really are."

"This is Judy Banks," she said. "I work for Harpo Productions, which produces *The Oprah Winfrey Show*."

Trying to sound professional, I asked for more details. By the end of the conversation, I was almost convinced Judy was who she said she was, but I told her I didn't watch talk shows, let alone *do* talk shows! (The few times in my life when I actually had time to watch daytime TV, the only talk show that impressed me happened to be *The Oprah Winfrey Show*.)

I told Judy I really didn't think I would be interested in being on the show, but thanks for asking. She ended the conversation with, "Think about it, and I'll call you tomorrow to see if you have changed your mind."

After hanging up and feeling a little stupefied, I called the few suspects left on my list who were brilliant enough to try to pull off this hoax. Their candid and innocent remarks convinced me that the joke really was on me. Yes indeed, I had just been extremely rude to a really nice lady from *The Oprah Winfrey Show.* But there was no way I would make a fool of myself on the number-one talk show in the nation, and I definitely did not want to face Judy Banks.

When I told my family and friends about the prospect of being on Oprah's show, I got comments like: "Why would she want you?", "Are you sure someone's not trying to pull your leg?", and "You should do it! You have a great story to tell!" My favorite comment was, "Awesome! But aren't you afraid you would choke on national television?"

My bishop said, "Helen, you for sure should do it! You have a great message you need to tell the world about." I still wasn't convinced.

The next day the phone rang and I checked the caller ID. There it was in digital letters: "Harpo Productions." I swallowed nervously, ignored the ringing, and quickly turned off our answering machine. During the day I decided that if they called back and if they would let me bring my husband and oldest son, I would consider doing the show.

So when they called a third time, with nervous trepidations I committed to be one of Oprah's guests. A week later we—my husband, son, and I—were on a first-class flight to Chicago. When a limousine picked us up at the airport, I knew this was for real. We stayed in a five-star hotel and ate the finest cuisine. Our family loves to camp, so Motel 6 would have been a luxury.

As we road through the streets of Chicago, I noted a stark contrast between the opulence of our limousine and the condition of the struggling street people we passed by. It weighed uneasily on my conscience and helped me appreciate my simple life in my hometown of Midway, Utah.

On our second day in Chicago, the limo picked us up early to take us to the studio. It was fascinating to see firsthand how Oprah's shows are produced. They taped three shows that day, and I was amazed at the efficiency with which her crew accomplished the seemingly impossible.

During a commercial break, I was taken on the set, and it was a surreal feeling as the searing, brilliant lights momentarily blinded me. My breath caught and I wondered what I was thinking when I agreed to do this. I vaguely remember being grateful I didn't eat breakfast so I couldn't lose it on national television. I somehow made it onto the stage or what looked like a platform. I reminded myself to breathe and then searched the audience for my husband and son. Their familiar faces calmed my nerves just enough that I could face Oprah. She was perfection in a pale pink suit and flawless hair and makeup.

Leave it to Randy. He ended up sitting by a lady that ran Oprah's farm, and he made friends with both this lady and Oprah. He even invited Oprah to come to Utah, to ride horses in the Wasatch Mountains and to meet our wonderful neighbors. Can you imagine Oprah walking around Midway, Utah, asking some interesting questions? I felt a little slighted, because I never really had a chance to visit with Oprah "off air," as she was so busy that day.

Before the show, I had some concerns about sharing what I considered events of a spiritual nature. I was worried Oprah or her audience would make light of my family's experience. Therefore, I was greatly relieved when she said before introducing me, "Intuition, which I call the voice of God . . . is the inner voice, the higher part of yourself, God speaking to you at all times in little ways and in big ways." This helped me to relax and to realize that Oprah and her audience would respect the spiritual aspects of what I had to say. The next hour went by in a blur and I had no idea what I had said until I watched the show a few weeks later when it was aired.

After the show was over, I felt a little disappointed, because I didn't have a chance to tell the amazing parts of our story. But then again, Oprah's show was on intuition, and that was only a minor part of my family's experience. Now, if she had done a show on miracles, I could have shared with the world our incredible experiences of divine intervention.

We, therefore, offer this book as the rest of our story, not only for our own posterity, but also for those who need to hear a story of faith, love, and miracles. Divine intervention happens every day of our lives if we simply recognize that God is in charge.

RANDY

The themes for this book are faith and miracles—a rather tall order. We do not pretend to understand the depths and scope of faith, nor do we understand how or why miracles occur. We went to the *Encarta World English Dictionary* and found this definition for the term *miracle:* "An act of God, an event that appears to be contrary to the laws of nature and is regarded as an act of God." The second definition reads, "Amazing event: an event or action that is amazing, extraordinary or unexpected." Interestingly, these definitions describe what we witnessed firsthand.

While we may yet not completely understand these concepts, what we do know is that we were recipients of all of the above in quite a dramatic fashion, and we can at least write about and record some rather unusual events in our lives.

You will note as you read our book that both of us tell our story. We have been invited to speak to a number of youth and adult groups about our experience, and this seemed to be the format that worked for us.

Sharing our experiences with others is rewarding because it reminds us of a very special year in our lives that continues to impact us in positive ways every day. We knew we wanted to a least record our experiences for our own posterity, and as we began writing, it became obvious that others might enjoy and benefit as well. So here it is. We would love to hear from you, particularly about miracles you have experienced. You will find our contact information in our bio at the end of this book.

If our story helps you gain insight into your own life, or gives you a greater desire to hug and hold on to your spouse and kids (as many have told us they did after listening to our story), and to appreciate the gift of life each day, our efforts will be well justified.

CHAPTER ONE
Family

HELEN

Terror constricted my wildly beating heart. The plane shuddered and dove as I desperately clutched the sleeping child in my arms. I felt his soft cheek against mine as I cried out over and over, "Devon, I am so sorry! I am so very sorry!" It had been only six months since I had brought him into this world, and the thought of his life being cut short was terrifying and unacceptable. All nine people on board were about to leave this earthly existence in one blinding flash. "Please, God, help us!"

Cold fear took my breath away. The motor had quit, but terrible sounds were coming from the plane. We were about to crash in some mountainous region of Arizona. How could Julie have such presence of mind to tell each of us to make sure our seat belts were tight and to put our heads between our knees? Without power and with a frozen rudder, the plane shuddered so loudly I could not hear what Doug, our pilot, was saying to the FAA, or what Randy, flying copilot, said as he cried out loud to God. I tried frantically to block out this horrifying nightmare, thinking back to the day Devon was born.

"Come on Mom, you can push harder than that! I have to go to work in ten minutes!" This command reflected all the patience and understanding my eighteen-year-old daughter, Jessica, could muster. I wasn't sure if I felt like laughing out loud or shaking her, but I doubted that after pushing for nearly three hours I had the strength to do either. How could I explain to her between contractions that having a baby at this advanced age (I was all of forty and feeling ninety) was just a bit more difficult than when I delivered her? My other five babies had all been born with just a few pushes. I am not sure if my body was rebelling or if it had just forgotten what to do after so many years of not experiencing childbirth, or maybe this little boy we had been looking at on the ultrasound wasn't in any hurry to make his grand entrance.

I guess I should have known what a stubborn and valiant soul we were about to be blessed with. I suspect the doctor knew that I, Jessica, and probably the baby were getting a little tired of this "pushing scene" when he said, "We're going to have to give this baby a little help!" In spite of what seemed like five nurses and one six-foot 230-pound husband jumping on my stomach in an attempt to "help," it was not happening. I thought nothing else could surprise me until the doctor reached for some instruments he called forceps, but which looked like they could be used to flip twelve-inch pancakes. I thought Jessica's eyes would pop right out of her head when she saw them. In the middle of my hyperventilating, I wondered if it was such a good idea to have Jessica witness the birth of her youngest brother.

Finally, with just a few more contractions, Devon came screaming into this world. As I watched Jessica touch his tiny hands and saw the wonder in her eyes, I knew an eternal bonding between my eldest and youngest had just taken place. I looked at my husband fussing over his new son as he was being tortured with all the necessary but rude things that are done to a newborn in those first shocking moments of life outside the womb. I could see the pride in Randy's face and I fell in love with him all over again, as I have with the birth of each of our children. I gazed at this big, gentle man who had given me six beautiful children and realized that instead of my love being divided a little further with each addition to our family, my capacity for love had been multiplied. I was overwhelmed with the miracle of it all as I looked at this perfect little body that love had created.

The nurses gently wrapped Devon in soft blankets and handed him to me. "So you're the little guy so determined to come to our family," I whispered to this warm little bundle fresh from heaven. I have held each one of my children as newborns and looked into their wise eyes. There is a light there that seems to reflect their wordless knowledge of God and the pre-existence they just left. As I gazed at this precious new son, it was almost as if translucent, delicate threads still connected him to heaven.

Lying in the hospital after the birth of my son, my mind drifted back nine and a half months earlier. I thought of some of the experiences that prepared me to be blessed with this special little boy. Our family, along with several other families, was camping at Lake Powell in southern Utah. One night I had what I then called a terrifying nightmare. I dreamed I was pregnant, and I woke up sobbing uncontrollably.

The next day I sat on our friend's houseboat and talked to Julie, who had two little "cabooses" when her oldest children were in high school. I mentioned the dream to her and she very calmly said, "You know, Helen, it really wouldn't be that bad. You'd be surprised how much you would enjoy a baby now and how great it would be for your family. Our two little ones have really pulled our family together." I just laughed and gave a dozen or maybe a thousand reasons why having a baby then would be pure insanity. Of course I was too old. I had been twenty-nine for eleven years by then, which meant I would be the unthinkable age of forty in a couple of weeks. I couldn't seem to handle the children I had already (or maybe they couldn't handle me!).

My vision of a happy, organized, immaculate, scripture-reading family with perfect attendance at school, church, and community events, had—out of necessity for my sanity—been filed in the back recesses of my guilt-ridden mind, hopefully never to surface again. Now it seemed I had to be content if I could kick a path wide enough through the major areas of traffic that no one tripped and got seriously hurt. My neat and tidy laundry room lost its credibility after my first child was born. In recent years it had been mistaken as a collection bin for the local thrift store. I'm sure there was a washer and dryer in there somewhere; didn't I do ten loads a day? How could I possibly add a newborn baby's laundry to this pile?

So, I jabbered on to Julie, trying to convince her, or maybe to convince myself, why we were so sure our family was complete at five children. Why was it so difficult to get this dream off my mind during the next few weeks?

A few days after getting home from Lake Powell we had settled into our normal routine of washing clothes that were not dirty and kicking aisle-ways through the clutter. I scolded Ryan for some trivial thing he had done, and he looked up at me with tears in his eyes and in his sweet little six-year-old voice said, "Don't you want me anymore?" It broke my heart. I dropped to my knees, and feeling all of the guilt of the worst mother in the world, I gathered him in my arms, hugged him, and gave him the little "I love you but . . ." lecture we mothers are so good at.

That night I had a dream. A darling little blond boy came to me and said, "Don't you want me?" When I woke up I thought it was my youngest son, Ryan, in the dream, but it wasn't. The little boy looked similar to my boys, but I had never seen him before.

These experiences began to weigh heavily on my conscience. What if there really was another spirit meant to come into our family? Would I someday be in heaven and have to face this little spirit that I had disappointed? My rational mind told me that physically, mentally, emotionally, economically, etc., etc., having a baby— especially at this age—was not the sane thing to do. But my heart had a hard time putting it to rest.

A few weeks later as I was getting ready to go to a seminar at Brigham Young University, I thought, *I sure hope I don't get morning sickness while I'm there.* I stopped dead in my tracks. Where did that come from? Why would I even think that? I couldn't possibly be pregnant! That would be almost medically impossible! Sure, I had dropped in unexpectedly on Randy at his office for a little romantic interlude, but we were careful! (Since we had five children it was a little hard to get any alone time with my husband—I had to take what I could get.) He was out of town after that, so no way was I pregnant. I shook my head and passed it off as a brain misfire. We used to have a computer that, when it got overloaded, would pull a sentence out of who knew where that would make no sense at all. I was pretty sure my brain was on supermom-wanna-be overload.

A couple of days later as I was sitting at a traffic light, I started to cry. (Don't lots of moms cry at traffic lights?) It was too early for any of the telltale signs of pregnancy; I would have only been one week pregnant, but I positively knew I was carrying our sixth child. When I mentioned this to Randy he sputtered in complete innocence, "That's impossible!"

It came as no surprise a few weeks later, when I was in an elevator with some rather unusual smells (had all fifty people in that four-by-four-foot space forgotten to shower for the last month?) and nearly lost my lunch. I went straight to our local grocery store to pick up a home pregnancy test. I hid it under a loaf of bread in my grocery cart out of fear I would run into someone I knew. I was mortified when the checker yelled to the employee in the next aisle, "What's the price on this pregnancy kit?"

The next morning I read the results in stunned silence. Though I was somewhat of an emotional basket case at the prospect of having one more child, I was surprisingly happy about it. Probably because of the experiences I had over the last few weeks, I was not traumatized at the idea of being pregnant, like I had been in my dream.

However, I was concerned about how Randy, the children, and the rest of my world would take the news. In the past, I had looked at women in this predicament and thought, *How could they do that to themselves? How could they be so dumb?* In retrospect and with a repentant heart, I now thought, *How could they be so blessed and so very fortunate?*

At first, my ever-supportive husband, Randy, was in complete denial. He tried to pretend that he had nothing to do with it and that it was not his fault, but I think the burden of having one more child weighed heavily on his mind. With time he got used to the idea, and through the years has completely enjoyed his little buddy.

I was sure my teenage children would disown me when we told them I was pregnant, so we postponed the announcement for a while. Interestingly enough, the children were having their own preparatory experiences. It made me wonder if maybe Devon's little spirit was sneaking about, inspiring his soon-to-be siblings. During the next few weeks, the children each came to me, unbeknown to each other, with this brilliant idea that our family needed a baby. The clincher came at a Sunday dinner when our eighteen-year-old daughter announced, "Mom, I've been thinking about it, and I decided what this family needs is another baby. So, get on it!"

I glanced over at Randy as we each tried to pry our lower jaw off the table without anyone noticing. I doubt it came as any great surprise a few weeks later when we broke the news at a family meeting. All my children cheered and hugged me, except seventeen-year-old Jacob. Always my analytical and responsible child, he said anxiously, "Whoa, you can't afford the kids you have now." However, he quickly warmed to the idea, and once Devon was born, Jacob became the perfect big brother.

Over the next few months, it was interesting to watch the reaction of family and friends as we told them about the pregnancy. The reactions ranged from laughing, crying, faces turning pale, raised eyebrows, and mouths hanging open, to comments like "You still do that?", "I hope you're kidding," and "How did this happen?" (Duh!) My favorite comment was my saintly mother's, who said with tears in her eyes, "Oh, that is wonderful! I've been praying something really good would happen to your family!" And with that, she gave me the reassuring hug I so desperately needed.

At the time, I was not sure why Devon came into our lives when he did. If he was really meant to come to our family, why he didn't come sooner, before I was "over the hill"? Thinking back several years later, I realized he came to our family when we needed him the most. I believe the Lord knew we had some trying times ahead and that Devon's mission would be to keep us smiling and give us perspective. At first, it was difficult keeping up with him, as he had more passionate energy than our other five children combined, but not a day has gone by since his birth that he hasn't made me smile and laugh. He has been our light and anchor through the tumultuous and stormy times.

So, there I found myself in the hospital with all my profound thoughts. Mothers of brand-new babies often have profound thoughts. I used to wonder if it was from participating in the miracle of birth with the heavenly aura that surrounds a newborn, or if it was simply from the pain medication. Regardless, for me it was always a tender and euphoric time.

The next day, when I still felt spiritually high but was in excruciating pain, my doctor came in to check on me. He informed me that I may need surgery to correct problems caused by pushing so hard during Devon's birth. Of course, I did what any normal mother of a newborn would do—I burst into tears! To this, my wonderful and understanding doctor patted me on the back and asked, "What's the matter? Are we having postpartum blues?"

I stifled the urge to grab him around the neck, shake him, and scream, *"No! We are not having postpartum blues! I am perfectly in control of my emotions, and I want this pain to go away this second. So do something about it now!"* But since I didn't have the energy to do that, I just told myself to get a grip. Sure enough, within a year or two, I did.

There is nothing that really compares to bringing a newborn home, especially when you are forty. A forty-year-old does not function quite the same at 2:00 AM as a twenty-year-old does. My big shock was to find out that old bodies take infinitely longer to recuperate. I'm pretty sure they never do get back to normal. (Was mine ever normal anyway?) However difficult the adjustments of bringing a newborn into a family, the joys far exceed description. It is as if a mist of contentment infiltrates every corner of a home, bringing a refreshing and peaceful glimpse of heaven. The love Devon brought into our home was so tangible at times that I felt I could touch it with my hand. He very quickly wiggled his way into the heart of each of his siblings and bound our family together with love.

When Devon was a few weeks old, our family was sitting together in church. I looked down the row at my six golden-haired children, and it took my breath away. Jessica, sitting between Jacob and Brandon, was holding Devon. With looks of awe and wonder in their eyes, those three teenagers sat mesmerized, staring at their little brother through most of the meeting. I was so touched I began to cry. I figured the ward members sitting around us were probably thinking, *Yep, Helen has the baby blues.* (I was sure my doctor called some of the ward members to warn them that I was losing it and to watch for the signs.) I smiled through my tears, and in that moment I experienced a completeness I had never known. Any doubts, pain, or suffering that had come with bearing this child vanished and were replaced with an undeniable sense of contentment.

At times, having a newborn mixed in with all the activities of our other five children was scary. We only forgot the baby once, and it was due to a miscommunication of who was watching whom. I took Ryan to his t-ball game and left Randy in charge of Devon, who was sleeping in his crib. An hour later we all met at Brandon's baseball game. I walked up to Randy and asked him where the baby was. With a horrified look he said, "Don't you have him?" I stopped breathing and Randy turned pale, and we jumped in the car and raced home. We flew up the stairs and found our one-month-old sleeping peacefully in his crib. I started breathing again as I stroked his velvety soft hair and wondered how many more heart attacks we would experience while raising this child.

Little did I know that Devon's birth would not be the only miracle to happen to our family during the year. Who could have imagined that six months later I would say to this little infant and to my eleven-year-old daughter, "I'm so sorry!" as the private plane we sat in careened downwards towards the earth in a nighttime storm, without power and covered with ice.

CHAPTER TWO
Courtship

RANDY

Since women come from Venus and men from Mars, it seems natural for Helen to talk about the birth of our children, and for me to talk about the conception part.

Walking down University Avenue in Provo, Utah, on a hot June afternoon, I paused in the shade of a maple tree, and the idea came to me as clear as if a friend whispered in my ear, "Get your butt over to Denver and ask Helen to marry you. It doesn't matter that you only have $35 to your name. It doesn't matter that you and Helen just graduated from BYU and have no job, no place to live, no money, no plans. It doesn't matter that you have only known each other a little over eight weeks and were too busy to date much during your last semester. You have just found your best friend, your kindred spirit, and you are wildly attracted to her. Marry her!"

A good friend and former missionary companion, Rick Vernon, had told me it was revealed to him in the temple that he needed to get Helen and me together on a blind date—how could I say no to that? Now, a little fasting and prayer had opened the lines of heavenly communication and helped me receive a definitive answer. So, off I went to Colorado.

After driving all night and arriving in Denver at 4:00 AM, I was tired, but not so tired that I could not convince Helen to climb a mountain with me. At the summit I excused myself and returned with a bouquet of mountain flowers gathered together with a diamond wedding ring. She gasped and thought for a moment that it was fake, but not for long. She cried in both happiness and shock; she'd thought I'd come to town to break off our relationship. I said, "I wanted to surprise you. Will you meet me at the Manti Temple in six weeks for a wedding? I'll go to California and earn enough money for a good honeymoon. Can we have an evening reception at Snowbird Ski Resort?" (I had taught skiing there and loved the outdoor plaza.)

Helen said, "I'm busy that weekend." Before I fell over, she added, "We have a family reunion in Washington State that weekend, but I will marry you the following weekend. I'll get the reception planned, and you go to L.A. and earn enough money for the honeymoon and the first-month's rent for an apartment." We were together three days of our six-week engagement.

Our wedding happened as planned and we headed off to Jackson, Wyoming, for the first leg of our honeymoon. After a few nights in a nice cabin at Jackson Lake, we headed out for a backpacking excursion in the Grand Tetons. It was not the crisp, thin air at 10,000 feet, or the peaceful meadow encircled by tall pine trees, or the majestic peaks, or even the six-point elk that came crashing through our campsite that I remember most. No, what caught my attention was what awaited me in a backpacking tent, backlit with alpine glow: caramel fondue with fresh fruit packed by Helen, and T-bone steak and salad packed by me with dry ice for our first night. Other things awaited me in that warm tent.   Move forward about seven weeks. We were living in a small beach house in Hermosa Beach, California. I came home one evening from work to sit down to a nice meal prepared by my gourmet cook. After dinner, Helen brought out a rather large decorated cake. Using her art background, she had created a large stork carrying a little bundle. I said, "No way." She said, "Yes way."

So much for my theory of not getting pregnant on honeymoons! As near as we could calculate, our baby would come about nine and a half lunar months from, shall I say, a special night near the tops of the Grand Tetons. We both cried—mostly tears of joy, but a few tears of anxiety at the idea of becoming new parents. Because both of us had experienced health problems, we had been concerned we would not be able to conceive a baby. Little did we know how much love and joy (and sometimes pain) would come into our lives as a result of six such bundles of love.

I never imagined that eighteen years later our eldest daughter, Jessica—the stork's first bundle—would fly to Phoenix, Arizona, to comfort me as I lay in an intensive care unit. She and our other children would be our primary support during a difficult time.

CHAPTER THREE
Premonitions

HELEN

The year Devon was born, our family faced unusual stresses. The end of August we sent our firstborn off to college. What trauma! I had no idea how excruciatingly difficult it would be to dump her off at that crummy little student apartment. I remember thinking, *It's a good thing the Lord sent me Devon so I wouldn't have as much time to miss Jessica.*

As we drove off, leaving her there in the cold, cruel world, I thought, *Maybe this will be a good experience. Maybe she's had life too easy. Now she'll have to fend for herself and grow some.* As it turned out, the next two years would bring plenty of growth experiences, probably more than she would ever want.

After we got home from "dumping" our first daughter, our life settled into the usual chaotic routine. (I suppose one could say things returned to normal, but I doubt there is any such thing as far as the Hall family is concerned.)

I was worried about my seventeen-year-old son, Jacob. Two weeks before Devon was born, one of Jake's closest friends, Coleman, had died suddenly of a heart attack. This was a friend with whom, for the past six winters, Jake had spent nearly every weekend skiing or snowboarding. During the summers they went mountain biking, camping, hiking, waterskiing, or skateboarding.

One evening, Jake had gone with Coleman to a concert, and he'd planned to spend the night at Coleman's house but instead decided to come home. He told Coleman he would meet him in the morning and then left him at the concert with another friend. A few minutes later as Coleman was leaving the arena, he collapsed on the ground and died. Jake had come home and gone to bed, not knowing he had seen Coleman alive for the last time.

Early in the morning, I woke up Jake to break the sad news. I will never forget the look of devastation on his face and the pain in his eyes. As I held him in my arms and cried with him, his six-foot-three-inch muscular body shaking with anguish, I wondered if he would ever recover from this heartache. It was almost as if a light went out that would take years to be fully illuminated again. I watched him struggle through the funeral. He and his buddies were the pallbearers. I felt my heart would break for him as I watched him, looking so lonely and pale, help carry his friend's casket out of the chapel. After the funeral, school suddenly seemed so unimportant, and Jake had a hard time finishing the school year. During the summer he seemed to be doing a little better—to be coping with Coleman's death. However, once school started, I could see that Jake was having a hard time again. I suspected he was thinking about the upcoming snowboarding season and getting through it without Coleman. On top of all this, Jake had developed ulcers from taking too much ibuprofen for some back problems. He had been to a doctor, but nothing seemed to help. I often lay awake at night, concerned about Jake and wishing he could have the same carefree life I had experienced at his age.

Taking care of a baby, worrying about Jake, missing Jessica, and trying to meet the countless demands of a family of eight were not the only stresses zapping my energy. I had begun working about one hundred hours a week (or was it really just forty?) on my design business. I designed and produced character figures: Father Christmas, mountain men, and Native American dolls. Designing and producing the dolls turned out to be more work than I had anticipated. I knew my hands were just a little too full, especially with baby Devon in them most of the time. I hired a few employees and the situation became more manageable.

Randy was also having a tough year. He had been working for a new company, and it was not as promising as he had hoped. He was not earning enough money to support the family, so in the fall he quit his job with another job lined up. In the meantime we had no health insurance. I think as much as anything he was still having a hard time adjusting to not owning his own business. Since we had been married, we had always owned our own business. In 1991, we sold our cookie company, which had been listed in *Inc. 500* and was based in Los Angeles, and were planning on semi-retiring in Utah with Randy teaching college part time. However, the company that bought our business figured out a way to avoid making their agreed-upon payments. The buyers sold the assets, took the money, and walked away, leaving debts in our name.

The financial pressures put a great deal of strain on our family. This meant Randy would have to start another company or work for someone else. It seems to me that a man's self-esteem is greatly affected by how he is able to provide for his family. He took the loss of our business and his job struggles personally, and I could tell he was having a very rough time emotionally. We needed a break and we needed it soon.

It seemed that break would come in the form of an invitation from our friends Julie and Doug Wagstaff, who called one day to ask if we would like to fly with them in their private plane to Mazatlan, Mexico, and stay in their condo on the beach for a week. This seemed to be just what the doctor had ordered, and it was too good of an opportunity to pass up. There is nothing quite like lying in the warm sand, listening to the soothing sound of waves and soaking up a few rays, to calm the soul and bring a little peace to a hectic life. Living in the mountains of Utah, we found that nature can be very healing. We were hoping a peaceful ocean would do the same. Just the thought of going on this trip lifted our spirits and made the challenges in our lives so much more bearable.

RANDY

From the time we met, Helen and I discovered we had a common dream: to live in a high mountain valley surrounded by alpine peaks, and to raise our children in the country with horses and other animals. We discovered just such a place forty-five minutes northeast of Provo, Utah, in the Wasatch Mountains, in a small, Swiss-style village called Midway. To get to Midway, one drives from Provo through a beautiful canyon, passing by spectacular waterfalls with a backdrop of 11,000-foot peaks. We made the move even before we sold our cookie company, and I commuted to Los Angeles each week. I put in my sixty hours of work in four days, and then came home for a glorious three-day retreat every weekend. We did all the things one can do in the mountains: horseback riding, camping, fishing, hunting, snow skiing, hiking, mountain biking, and romping in the hills with our kids. We boated and waterskied in lakes just a few minutes away. We learned to grow a large vegetable garden under the tutelage of loving neighbors. There were times when I had to pinch myself to make sure it was reality and not a dream.

One of the great advantages of living in the country is meeting new friends with common interests and values. We quickly came to love the people and the families in our community. Living in a relatively crime-free community with neighbors who brought you fresh vegetables and homemade jam and bread seemed almost too good to be true. Shortly after we moved to Midway, our dog was involved in the biggest crime of the week. The headline for the local weekly newspaper read: "Horse Narrowly Escapes Injury when Cornered by a Golden Retriever and Black Labrador." The sheriff was unable to apprehend the dogs—apparently the dogs were too fast. This was quite a contrast to the front-page crime stories of Los Angeles. In L.A., most crimes did not even make the newspapers.

Before long we became friends with Doug and Julie Wagstaff and their eight children. It was not their airplane, their horses, or their talent at running a restaurant, catering weddings, and running their marine resort at the lake that intrigued us. It was not Doug killing me in racquetball, how he cruised the channel at Lake Powell at eighty-five miles per hour, or how well their kids did in sports and other school activities that impressed us. What impressed us most was their family motto of "work hard and play hard," their commitment to their faith, and their kindness to our family. Our boys worked for the Wagstaffs at their lake resort. Going to work in a bathing suit, working with watercraft, teaching waterskiing and wakeboarding, and working with snowmobiles in the winter was a dream for my sons—a dream I knew I would have to awaken them from at some point to introduce them to the real world.

At any rate, we were thrilled at the opportunity to fly to Mazatlan with the Wagstaffs and to spend a week with them there. It seemed like the perfect thing for us to do at this time of transition. We were just not prepared for the trauma that would happen next.

HELEN

As excited as I was about going on this trip, I also had mixed feelings. I had lain awake several nights worrying about flying to Mexico in the Wagstaffs' plane. This was unusual for me, as I have always enjoyed flying. My father owned several planes and I loved flying with him. When I was a little girl, he would put me on his lap and let me hold the yoke, so I thought I was flying the plane all by myself. I remember the thrill of looking down at the "toy" cars and houses, surrounded by tiny farms with miniature, grazing cows. As we flew over majestic mountains and glorious vistas, I'd think how wonderful it would be to be a bird and witness these spectacular views every day of my life. Back then, I dreamed of one day owning my own plane and flying around the world.

For some reason, however, the thought of getting on the Wagstaffs' plane terrified me. I felt a very real fear—almost a premonition—that we would crash. Several of my close friends had similar feelings; one friend even mentioned this to me in tears. Yet other friends and my husband all made positive comments, such as: "There is nothing to worry about," and "Flying is safer than driving on the freeway." The most interesting comment had to be, "It's a sign of depression if you are afraid to do anything. You must really need this trip." All in all, I reminded myself that Doug was an exceptional pilot with over 3,000 hours of flying time and that he was instrument rated. In addition, this was a larger plane than, say, a single-engine Cessna.

After praying about it several times, the feeling came very strongly to me that everything would be all right, that it would be for our best, and that it would be okay to go on the trip. I made the decision to go, yet I still worried. The scripture "If ye are prepared ye shall not fear" kept running through my head. So how could I prepare myself? To my "get ready" list, I added: check on insurance policy, mail tithing check, and attend the temple before we go. On my "things to take" list I put matches, flashlight, and a water container in case we crashed in the deserts of Mexico. So now that I was totally prepared I would no longer have to worry, right? Wrong.

I would find out later I was not the only one to have premonitions about this trip. The night before we left, we went to a local restaurant for dinner. While there, we ran into some friends of ours. The wife, Shari, with a pained look on her face, ducked her head and would not talk to us. I wondered all through dinner about her strange reaction to seeing us, and I worried that one of my "angelic" offspring had done something to offend her. A month later, she told me she couldn't look at or talk to me for fear she would burst into tears. She was sure we would think she was nuts. She had asked the Wagstaffs to take a bag of clothing to her son who was on an LDS Church mission in Mazatlan. She told us that as she packed that bag, she had the distinct impression the bag would never make it to her son. Every time she put her hand in the bag it would make her cry. For several days before our trip, she had wanted to call the Wagstaffs or us and beg us not to go. She decided that in addition to confirming her craziness, it would do no good. So, not knowing of her premonitions, I continued to wonder about my own.

The last few days before our trip were filled with the usual frenzy that hits before a vacation. We would be taking six-month-old Devon, since he was still nursing, and eleven-year-old Maryann to help babysit. We were leaving our three sons—seventeen-year-old Jake, fifteen-year-old Brandon, and seven-year-old Ryan—at home to fend for themselves. We had warned the neighbors to watch for wild parties and the-parents-are-out-of-town celebrations. Jessica was in southern Utah attending college.

The Friday before we left, I insisted Randy check into our life insurance policy and make sure we were current on our payments. I was concerned that our policy might have lapsed during our recent financial crunch.

The next day at a baptism at our church, I mentioned my concerns to a friend, who I knew had flown in the Wagstaffs' plane many times and was a pilot himself. He said, "Oh, you don't have a thing to worry about. You are flying with Doug, and he has 3,000 hours flying time." I felt somewhat appeased, and the prospect of being in the warm Mexican sun was sounding better all the time.

The last few days before leaving, I was madly trying to finish a large Father Christmas order. Early one morning I was working in my workshop, a room in the upper level of Randy's parents' home. Devon was with me. Whenever anyone would walk into the room and talk to him or give him any attention, he would get very excited, giggle, and jabber back. Devon was sitting on my lap when he looked towards the doorway. Suddenly, his little body trembled with excitement and he began eagerly jabbering to someone in the hallway. I thought Wilma, a friend that worked for me, must have just walked in. I turned around to greet her and was surprised to see an empty hallway. I looked at Devon, who I could swear was still chatting to someone. I walked out into the hallway and called out, "Who's there?" No response. I felt a little silly as I asked Devon, "Who are you talking to?" It was one of those moments when your heart rate kicks up a notch or two and you wonder, *What was that?* Though it was an eerie experience at the time, it wouldn't make sense until I thought of it again a few years later.

CHAPTER FOUR
Flight

HELEN

Before we walked out the door, we sat our six children down for a few last-minute instructions and our traditional family prayer. I'm sure my tears were a reminder to my husband of my concerns, so after the prayer, Randy said bluntly, "If anything should happen to us, we have a life insurance policy, and we would want you to live with Aunt Linda and Uncle Owen." (Of course, we had not informed Linda and Owen of this proposition—wouldn't they be surprised to double their family?) I looked at the horrified expressions on the children's faces and then glared at Randy with that "What are you doing?" look.

With tears in her eyes, Jessica turned to me and asked, "Why is Dad saying this?"

"Oh, no reason," I answered. "It's just a good idea to be prepared." My voice cracked as I added unconvincingly, "We'll be just fine!"

Jessica's return comment, "With all the trips you and Dad have gone on, you've never talked like this!" rang a little too true.

In the driveway, we hugged the children goodbye and told them we loved them and to take good care of each other. I was a little concerned about Jessica, who was leaving at the same time to drive alone the four hours back to school. She and I would cry every time she left for college. I still had some pretty hefty apron strings with lots of secure knots holding my firstborn. With the usual unrestrained tears, I kissed her goodbye and we left for the airport. I suppose if I had any idea what the next twenty-four hours would bring, we would not have gone. Yet, knowing what we learned by going on the trip, I don't know if I would trade the experience for the safety of staying home.

As we drove the five minutes to our small local airport, I saw my tithing check in my purse and realized I had forgotten to mail it. *Oh, well,* I thought, *I can mail it tomorrow in Tucson, Arizona.* I also noticed a few high, non-threatening clouds that reminded me of a recent winter storm that had moved south—a rather severe storm for November. I thought, *Wait a minute, aren't we flying south? Oh, well, Doug knows what he is doing, and if we have to drop down and wait out a storm, so be it.*

RANDY

The sleek, bright red A36 turbo-charged Bonanza aircraft contrasted sharply against the blue afternoon sky and white, fluffy clouds. The plane was loaded with features, including a Loran computer, autopilot, and a heated prop for de-icing. I suppose it gave us a false sense of security as we stepped into the lush interior. Doug and I sat in the pilot and copilot seats. I've flown a little, but I am not a pilot. I asked Doug a few questions, such as how to raise and lower the landing gear, then settled in for the first leg of the flight to Mexico.

Julie, who was four months pregnant, sat across from Helen in the back of the plane. The club seating meant that the two rows of seats actually faced each other. Six-month-old Devon would ride on Helen's lap. Our eleven-year-old daughter, Maryann, sat directly across from Helen and Devon. The Wagstaffs' ten-year-old daughter Robyn, five-year-old son Brandon, and two-year-old daughter Brittany came along as well. We had two capable young girls to help watch the young children; it sounded like a great idea to me.

Julie had told us to pack light, and even with the five children, we were at or under the maximum weight allowance for the plane. Everyone seemed to have ample room. Later, the media would need something to say for their lead story, so they picked up on someone saying we were overloaded and were over the plane's weight allowance. It is interesting how people in the media report hearsay as if it were fact.

HELEN

As we headed down the runway, I wondered if my heart was pounding so fast from extreme excitement or just plain fear. I remember the elation I felt every time I took off with my dad in one of his planes, headed for another adventure. This time it was more of a chilling, gnawing sensation.

Once we were airborne, I asked Julie what the weather forecast was for our flight plan. She said she didn't know and that Doug would use his radio to find out soon. My heart skipped a beat and I had to catch my breath, as something felt out of sync.

I recalled waiting in my dad's car while he would go into the airport terminal to get the latest weather report before we got in the plane. He always did that. I remember once when my mom said to him, "You can see the sky is perfectly clear, and the weather report when we left home was good. We are only flying a few miles. Surely you don't have to waste time calling now." To this, my father replied, "I never take off without knowing exactly what I am flying into."

The butterflies in my stomach yanked me back to the present. I tried to appease my fear by telling myself, *Well, when he radios in for the report, if there is a problem we can just turn back.* Who would have known he would be given an inaccurate, sketchy report?

The cabin of the plane was soon full of conversation about the upcoming week in Mazatlan, and that and the thrill of flying momentarily drowned out my anxiety. Julie explained all the fun things we would be doing in Mazatlan. When she told me about an experience from her family's Mexico trip the previous year, the butterflies came winging right back to my stomach. It turns out that while in Mexico the previous November, the Wagstaffs had decided one day to go flying to see the beautiful coastline. After they got the plane in the air, the oil pressure started dropping dramatically. Doug managed to fly the plane safely back to the airport in Mazatlan, but they ended up having to fly home commercially, leaving the plane in Mexico to get a new engine. Julie's only comment about the trip was, "You know, I didn't feel comfortable about that trip from the beginning."

I suppose Julie noticed the color draining from my face, or the beads of perspiration accumulating on my forehead, because she casually asked, "Are you all right?"

I answered as calmly as I could, "Uh, oh . . . sure. Tell me, were you at all uneasy about this trip?"

With a peculiar look on her face she said, "No, not at all." Later, I learned that the Wagstaffs had also gone over their insurance information with their children before leaving on the trip. They had never done that before either.

Trying to act calm and unconcerned, I opened the two-pound bag of peanut M&Ms Julie had brought to pacify the children. Whenever I have to face life's challenges, I always seem to do it better with chocolate in my hands. My husband likes to say, "Give Helen her daily dose of M&Ms and she's a happy woman." I practically gulped down a large helping of the candy as I sat on the plane, but for once the chocolate failed to calm my troubled nerves.

As we soared through a glorious crimson sunset, the saying "Red sky in the morning, sailors take warning. Red sky at night, sailors delight!" buzzed through my head. Or was it "Red sky in the morning, pilots take warning. Red sky at night, don't take the flight"? I felt a little claustrophobic as the sunset faded and night fell.

RANDY

Our destination for the first night was a warm hotel in Tucson, Arizona. After takeoff from the Heber City Airport, we flew south over the Wasatch Mountains. The first half of the flight was smooth, and the conversation was happy and relaxed. As evening approached and we crossed over Lake Powell on the Utah–Arizona border, the clouds grew thicker and darker. I looked down at the massive power plant near Page, Arizona, on the shores of the lake. How many times had we passed by the plant in a speedboat? The familiarity gave me some security, but I could not help but think how nice it would be to set down at the airport in Page. I almost told Doug my thoughts.

As we continued south, we encountered more clouds, more turbulence. The rain began to machine-gun the plane, and we started bouncing, or, as I like to call it, rockin' and rollin'. Doug wisely contacted the FAA at Albuquerque Central (AC) and filed an IFR (instrument flight rules), as we were still flying VFR (visual flight rules). He also requested the weather report for Tucson, which was "8,000-foot ceiling and showers." I believe I heard the report with my earphones. Doug suggested we bring up closer airports on the Loran for a possible early landing. Doug and I both tried to check several different airports. The Loran indicated we were forty minutes from Tucson at our present rate of speed, which was about 230 miles per hour. Without speaking to each other, Doug and I came to a silent consensus to push on to Tucson. Doug mentioned that most of the closer airports were in mountainous areas and may not have lights. He had flown in rain and clouds before, and with ample instrumentation there should not have been a problem with an 8,000-foot ceiling in Tucson.

Conditions continued to deteriorate. Rain pummeled the plane. It was now dark, and the heavy rain clouds allowed no visibility. I pictured a tin can blowing in the wind and rain on a dark, cold night, only it was our plane and not a can. I had flown a lot, and I could never remember bouncing, shuddering, and being tossed this much. I've been in massive turbulence on commercial planes, and I used to chuckle and wonder why people panicked. But it was panic time for me now. I could literally feel fear in my chest. I told my heart to keep beating and my brain to keep functioning, because Doug needed me. It got worse. There was no question we were at war with a violent storm. We were told later that this was one of the worst November storms in Arizona's history, and that we probably had fifty- to sixty-mile-per-hour crosswinds.

Julie and Helen were acutely aware of what was happening. I faintly heard them utter a vocal prayer on our behalf. I was told that the kids prayed, too. About this time, I remember Julie leaning over our chairs and saying to Doug, "Tell me straight. I need to know what is happening." Doug said that it was quite rough but we would be okay, and that we were thirty-six minutes out of Tucson. I was not quite so confident, but I thought prayer might give me more peace. I pleaded with the Lord and felt some comfort. It was a little like putting on another coat in a storm—the storm still feels incredible, but one feels warmer inside. It also gave me more hope.

Doug got back on the radio with Albuquerque Central and said, "We're in a mess up here. What should we do?" Central instructed Doug to climb from our present altitude of 9,500 feet to 11,500 feet. I think the assumption was that we could get above the storm. Doug pulled back on the yoke and I felt the plane begin to climb. I could hear the motor straining, and as the plane continued to climb I watched Doug reach down, pick up a flashlight, and shine it on the wing. To our absolute horror, we saw ice on the wings. At this higher elevation, we were experiencing ice and snow. Doug handed me the flashlight and said, "What have we got?" I scanned the wing on my side of the plane and reported that there was about an eighth of an inch of ice on top of the wing, but it looked like a quarter to a half inch on the front of the wing.

I had a horrible thought at this time: *I wonder how thick the ice needs to be before we lose our air lift and go down—a half inch, an inch? Maybe if I can still see the Phillips-head screws under the ice on the wing, we will keep flying.* We scanned the wings again. I remember fussing with the flashlight when suddenly the engine coughed once or twice and then resumed a normal pitch.

Doug yelled, "What the heck was that? I have never heard this plane do that!" My heart nearly stopped. Then Doug got back on the radio and, in a much more demanding tone, said loudly, "It's a mess up here. We've iced up and we are experiencing tremendous turbulence. We need to get back down!" I looked at the Loran, which indicated that at our current rate of speed, we should arrive in Tucson in twenty-seven minutes. I offered a prayer of thanksgiving every time I looked down to see a smaller number on the Loran. We could make it, maybe.

HELEN

I remember thinking, *Okay, all I have to do is count to 60 thirty times, and then we will be there.* I had visions of leaping out of our safely landed plane, dropping to my knees, and gratefully kissing the ground. I had already promised myself there was no way I was getting back on this plane in the morning to finish our flight to Mazatlan.

Julie kept saying, "Helen, I am so sorry. It's never like this. I'm so sorry to put you through this." It was typical of Julie; she is always concerned about others. And though she meant to make me feel better, her words only intensified my fears. I felt like I couldn't breathe from the absolute terror of the situation. The next few agonizing minutes tediously ticked by. We had another prayer with the children, pleading with the Lord to protect us.

The windows iced over and I felt like we were enclosed in a dark tomb. I knew Doug and Randy were checking the ice on the wings. Could it get worse? It could.

In a heart-stopping second, our worst possible nightmare became our living reality. The engine coughed two or three more times and then quit, leaving behind an ominous silence. The entire plane made a terrible, vicious noise, shaking violently. We were in a steep right dive.

Doug banged and jammed the yoke back and forth, trying to get the plane to glide. The sound reverberated off every bone and muscle in my body. When the engine quit, we were all thrown forward; we probably dropped from 230 miles per hour to somewhere in the 100's. It was like hitting the brakes hard while driving a car downhill. Doug somehow freed one hand, got back on the radio, and said, "Nine mike papa two seven zero. Uh, I just lost everything, all my controls! I'm in trouble here. Uh ... uh ... I ... I've really lost it here. I've lost all rudder control. The engine is not operating!" This was Doug's last radio communication taken word for word from the FAA accident report.

Sometimes words in the English language cannot even begin to convey an emotion. How would one describe the sensation of slipping while climbing a sheer rock face and then cascading downward? How would one describe the emotion felt while falling through the air, knowing death was imminent? I suppose "frozen with fear" and "sheer terror" come closest to describing my feelings as I realized the plane was crashing. As the gravity of the situation overwhelmed me, I could scarcely breathe. I knew that in a few minutes, my life and that of my husband and two of our children would end. Our good friends would die with us. Time slowed and seemed to take on a whole new dimension, but my mind kicked into overdrive. I cried silently to the Lord, begging for a chance to live, a chance to do better.

I closed my eyes and thought of the implications of our impending deaths. The idea of my four children at home, left behind and alone, with no parents and losing two siblings, was unbearable. I heard myself cry out, "Dear God, please don't let this happen to my children. I want to live! They need us!"

It is amazing how quickly life can be thrown into perspective. When facing death, all I really cared about was my family, the other people I love, and my beliefs. All of a sudden all the mundane daily activities, material wealth and possessions, the trivial things we spend ninety percent of our time on, seemed so ridiculously unimportant.

I thought of my daughter Jessica, and how in a split second her life would be destroyed. Being the oldest she would naturally feel the brunt of the responsibility for her siblings. Could she bear this heavy burden? Could she set aside her plans for the future?

I thought of Jacob, my seventeen-year-old son, and the horrified look on his face when I had to inform him, six months earlier, of his friend's death. He had not yet recovered from that loss. How could he possibly survive losing half of his family?

I pictured my fifteen-year-old son Brandon, so athletically gifted. I wanted to see him play sports again. He was planning to try out for the high school basketball team the next day. His dreams would be shattered in an instant.

What about sweet, angelic Ryan, the contented child who never complained? Would he ever be happy again? Can a seven-year-old ever really recuperate from the deaths of both parents?

I looked at Julie's kids and then at my innocent daughter, Maryann, sitting across from me. I could tell she was praying, and I admired her faith and courage. She was so talented and beautiful; surely her life had many more opportunities and adventures yet to unfold. She had so much to offer.

The most difficult thing of all was to look down at my six-month-old baby boy, who slept in my arms. I was amazed that he could sleep through this terror, but I guess the safety of a mother's arms is all a baby needs to block out awful noise and destruction. As I held him tightly to me, kissing his soft, sweet-smelling cheek and stroking his downy head, I whispered over and over, "I'm so sorry. I'm so very sorry." We had such a tough time bringing him into this world—he was a living miracle—and now we were going to take him out of this world. Yet, I had a distinct impression that this tiny son still had a mission to fulfill. "Please, dear God, let him live that he might fulfill his divine destiny," I prayed.

It is strange the thoughts you think at times of extreme stress. I had often wondered what people think about when they know they are going to die. Now I know. I wondered if I should wake Devon and nurse him so that going down so quickly would not make his ears pop—as if a little earache would hurt more than being crushed or torn to bits in an airplane crash. I remembered the tithing check in my purse and thought, *I hope someone finds it in the wreckage and mails it for me so I will be square with the Lord. Will someone even find the wreckage?* I thought about all the repenting I should be doing and wondered how effective deathbed repentance is. I made all sorts of promises if we survived: I would read the scriptures more, keep all the commandments, be a better wife, mother, and friend. In short, I wanted another chance to take a shot at perfection!

The seconds dragged on as I thought of my children at home. Would they soon be orphaned? Suddenly, a somewhat calming feeling washed over me. Our family still needed to be together in this mortal life, working out our eternal salvation.

Just then, Julie told everyone to make sure their seatbelts were tight, and she told the children to put their heads down and cover them with their arms. Julie exhibited an amazing courage and focus that would carry us through the coming days and weeks.

CHAPTER FIVE
Impact

RANDY

If the humming of the engine had calmed my nerves and provided a glimmer of hope, the-now silent engine opened up the very doors of hell, introducing me to a darkness and a state of helplessness no human being should ever visit. For a brief moment, it was as if time ceased to exist and I ceased to live, almost like I was a time traveler frozen somewhere in another dimension, trying to come back to the here and now. But the here and now was so filled with horror that for a moment I thought I might peacefully pass out.

When I realized we were at 10,000 feet and the ground was probably around 2,000 feet, I figured we had about eight to ten minutes to live. The region north of Tucson is mountainous, so I assumed we would crash into a mountain. Due to the darkness and the thick cloud cover, we had no visibility. All we could see were dark clouds, and ice covering the windows. We were incased in a deadly tomb. Loaded down with ice, the plane was dropping at a high speed and would disintegrate when it hit the ground.

No one survives a plane crash at night in a storm! I decided that I had enjoyed a good life and that death would not be so bad; there was nothing I could do about it anyway. Then I remembered my wife and two children in the back of the plane and thought, *No! We can't take them out like this!*

I prayed hard, asking Heavenly Father what I could do to help. I felt impressed to stay alert and even to wipe the windows for Doug. Because we were dropping so fast without power, they had fogged a little. I looked for any signs of the ground. We broke out of the clouds for just a few seconds and I told Doug I could see a few lights in the distance out the left window. Then we were back in the clouds and could only see darkness.

Doug did not try to veer the plane towards the lights. I believe he was inspired to keep the plane gliding straight at just the right speed. Too slow and the plane would stall and then go into a dive, too fast and it would fall apart upon landing. This focus may have saved our lives. Pilots who try to over-steer a gliding plane as they near the ground are usually killed in the process.

After seeing the lights about a thousand feet below us, I came to the awful realization that we had less than a minute to live.

What happened next is sacred to us, and at first we were reluctant to share it with anyone except our closest family and friends. We have since realized that most people appreciate spiritual events, and that someone might benefit from hearing this story. We believe the following experience explains why any of us survived the plane crash.

An overwhelming feeling came over me that without divine intervention, we would all perish in the next minute. Lightweight planes do not hold together when they hit mountains at 100-plus miles per hour (gliding speed for this plane with heavy ice). Ever since I received the Aaronic Priesthood at the age of twelve, I believed that if I were ever in great peril, I could call on God through His priesthood and He would deliver me from evil or a precarious situation. I didn't plan it, but when I felt the plane was nearing the mountains, I found myself raising my right arm and saying in a distinct voice, "In the name of Jesus Christ and by the power of the priesthood, I command this aircraft to protect its passengers."

I do not remember anything after that, since on impact I was knocked unconscious, critically injured and bloodied with a broken neck, a broken back, a broken tailbone, several broken ribs, a broken leg, and plenty of gashes. I also had short-term amnesia.

HELEN

I knew we would hit the ground any second. My last recollection was the stall buzzer going off. I knew that, one way or another, this nightmare was about to end. I do not recall the actual impact, as I was knocked unconscious. Julie, the only adult to remain conscious, remembers the plane hitting the ground just seconds after the stall buzzer sounded.

From the FAA report: "The aircraft made initial contact with the top of a 20-foot saguaro cactus, cutting off the top foot of the cactus. [The propeller hit the cactus. If the wing had hit the cactus, the plane probably would have cartwheeled, killing us all.] The aircraft then struck ground on upsloping terrain, leaving two ground scars [observers called them craters] on a heading of 340 degrees. [An antenna was found in the first ground scar, and the broken tip of a propeller blade was found at the second scar.] The aircraft came to rest 258 feet from the initial point of contact. The fuselage was resting on a heading of 058, with part of the horizontal stabilizer embedded in another saguaro cactus."

The plane hit a Palo Verde tree and spun around before imbedding itself in the saguaro, facing the opposite direction from its initial impact. The report states that the front of the plane was nearly torn off, with the cowling lying on the ground nearby and the motor hanging out in the dirt. Much of the plane was crushed, but the cabin held together and saved our lives. The major damage occurred to the front of the plane.

One of the Civil Air Patrol rescuers would later say, "No one could land a plane without power, in this terrain in broad daylight in perfect weather, and expect to have any survivors."

Doug never lowered the landing gear; had he done so, the plane probably would have flipped. We had zero visibility, but just before we hit the ground, for some reason Doug pulled back on the yoke and lifted the nose of the plane. This caused the stall buzzer to go off just before we hit on upsloping terrain. According to another observer, "Had Doug not pulled back on the yoke, the plane would have been in a hundred pieces, and so would you." When all he could see was darkness, why would Doug pull back on the yoke to raise the nose of the plane at just the right second? We believe his hands were guided by a higher power.

I do not remember the impact. All I could comprehend was darkness, pain, and confusion, as if awakening in a bad dream. My neck had an odd shape to it, and I felt something warm running down my forehead. I was having trouble breathing, couldn't move my arm, and was missing a tooth. I begged the fog in my brain to clear, and willed my stiff body to move. My motherly instincts kicked in and I knew I should have my baby in my arms, but he was missing. I cried out, "Where's my baby? Where is Devon?" and began groping frantically in the dark. At this point I was not coherent enough to know where I was or what had happened. I was vaguely aware of someone helping me.

I found a little foot and said, "Is this Devon?"

A voice answered back, "No, that's Brandon." Next I grabbed a little leg.

"No, that's Brittany." Was that Julie's voice I recognized?

I continued my desperate search, screaming, "Why isn't Devon crying? Dear God, help me find my baby." A few short minutes seemed like an eternity.

Julie climbed up over the back of her seat, moved some luggage, and climbed into the cockpit, where she could see Devon's little white Reeboks sticking straight up in the air. He was wedged so tightly between Doug's shoulder and the front of the cockpit that it took several good tugs to free him. Doug and Randy were unconscious at this time; no sound or movement was coming from the cockpit and we feared the worst. Julie delivered the now-screaming Devon into my arms. I hugged him with my good arm. He seemed to be all right. His only injury would come later when the nurse dropped him on the x-ray table and bruised his head. Sometime later, I realized that the only way for him to survive being thrown through the interior of the plane, through the luggage compartment, landing in front of our critically injured pilot on a jagged metal and plastic dashboard, would be for an unseen heavenly being to bear him up. (When Devon was two and a half years old, we had not yet told him what happened to him in the plane crash. One day, while he heard us talking about the crash, he said, "Oh, was that the time the angels were holding me?" Through the years, I have come to know who one of those angels was.)

I don't remember exactly what happened after I found Devon, since I was injured and probably in shock, but one thing I knew for sure was that I smelled gas and feared there would be an explosion or fire. I vaguely recall yelling for everyone to get out and get away. I was still delirious and thought we had been in a car crash. At this point, Doug and Randy were both unconscious. Luckily, it was dark and we could not see their bloody heads, or the blood that was splashed throughout the cockpit. We had no idea how many broken bones they had received from that initial impact. Thankfully, the five children, while shaken, seemed all right and could move just fine. We did not know that Maryann had a fracture in her back, and that the ever-strong and helpful Julie had hairline fractures in both legs. She would find out about the fractures later.

I was still somewhat incoherent as we scrambled out of the plane, landing in cacti and the unforgiving desert terrain. In total confusion I held onto Julie and asked her what had happened. "What? A plane crash?" I didn't even remember getting on a plane! Slowly my brain allowed the shocking reality to seep in. We had just survived a plane crash, and we were still in serious trouble. It was raining hard and the wind was blowing. After wandering around in the dark, the children getting pricked by cactus needles, Julie and I realized that if the plane was going to burst into flames it would have happened by now. The rain had obviously prevented any fires. With the gas spilled all around, a fire would have probably killed us all. Were we being protected from above?

As we climbed back into the plane, Maryann said, "Mom, why did this happen to us? We said a prayer!" And then I said something that sounded strange even to me. "We're alive—I don't know now, but I promise you that someday down the road we will understand the reason why this happened, and somehow it will turn out to be a blessing." I am sure she must have thought her mother was crazy. She looked at me with my head at an odd angle, blood running down my face, a missing front tooth, and unable to use my arm. The poor girl must have been thinking, *My dad and Doug are dying and my mom's a mess. She thinks this is going to be a blessing?*

We comforted the children as best as we could. They were amazingly brave. It was almost as if they knew the gravity of the situation required it. They were wet and cold from stumbling around outside the plane, but they were strong and didn't complain. They sat in stunned silence, trusting Julie and me to make everything all right. We found the baby blankets I had packed and huddled together in the cabin of the plane while we poured our hearts out to God, praying for help.

Doug woke up but was incoherent and delirious. He was wedged tightly between his seat and the dashboard. He kept begging us to help him into a warm Jacuzzi. After repeated pleadings he said, "If you won't help me into a Jacuzzi will you at least bring me a bowl of hot water?" For the next three hours he would mumble and moan sentences that made no sense. It gave us some comfort knowing that if he kept talking, he was still alive. He called out to his teenage sons, who were back home, saying, "Come on, Scott or Jon! Get up here and help me! You know I would help you if you needed it. I don't see why you won't help me!" I remember thinking that I hoped someday we'd be able to laugh about the crazy things he was muttering. I was impressed with how calm Julie remained and how she kept talking to Doug, trying to bring him around.

A couple of days after the crash I asked Julie, "How did Randy get out on the wing? Was he ejected out of the plane during the crash?"

Dumbfounded, she looked at me and said, "Helen, are you serious? You don't remember? You helped me lift him out onto the wing. You seemed perfectly cognizant. Boy, I'm sure glad I didn't know you weren't really with me! I would have been scared to death if I thought I was on my own."

Apparently, when Julie and I first opened the door of the cockpit to see what we could do to help our husbands, I saw Randy's bloodied and broken body and went into shock. I blocked out the following scene so completely from my mind that it was years before I could remember it.

Doug and Randy kept flailing their arms around and bumping into each other. We assumed they had broken bones and we knew they needed to be stabilized. Julie suggested we lay Randy on the wing of the plane and give Doug more room to stretch out. This may have saved them from any paralysis due to their broken backs and Randy's broken neck. By now Randy was more coherent and could mumble things to us. We encouraged him to help lift himself as we moved him to the wing of the plane. Julie found a tarp and wrapped Randy tightly in it to keep the rain off him, keep him somewhat warm, and keep him from moving.

Then, Julie tinkered with the radio to try to make contact with the FAA, but the radio equipment was dead. Surely the FAA was aware we had gone down, and they were waiting for contact, or looking for us. To say Julie was frustrated at this time would be an understatement. Why wouldn't anything work? Were the batteries dead? She went to the back of the plane and searched for emergency equipment. This may have been too much even for Julie—I could not see her tears in the dark, but mine ran freely. Was someone looking for us? Did they have any idea where we were? Would our husbands live through the night?

We thought we lost Doug twice during the night when he became very quiet. At one point I called out to Randy on the wing and said I thought we might be losing Doug. I asked Randy what we could do. To our surprise, he instructed Julie to lay her hands on Doug's head so he could give him a priesthood blessing from his position on the wing. Randy told me later that he had remembered a prophet telling his wife to lay her hands on another person's head for a blessing. Randy then proceeded to give Doug a blessing, telling him that he would live, that competent help would be on the way and would assist him. I was deeply touched at Randy's love and concern for his friend when Randy himself was in excruciating pain and, as it turned out, had the most critical injuries. I doubted either Randy or Doug would survive the night if we were not rescued soon.

As Randy struggled to breathe as he lay on the wing of the plane, I realized how much I truly loved this man. If he were to die I knew my life would cease to exist, for I couldn't possibly go on without him. I pleaded with the Lord to spare his life and give him strength to hold on until help came.

RANDY

Beryl Markem was the first woman to fly west across the Atlantic Ocean to North America, but her plane ran out of gas and crashed on the shores of New England. She waited to be rescued and would later describe the situation this way: "The silence that belonged to the slender little craft was, I thought, filled with malice—a silence holding the spirit of wanton mischief, like the quiet smile of a vain woman exultant over a petty and vicious triumph." I looked at our vile, crumpled aircraft and had similar thoughts.

It was now dark and quiet, except for the sound of rain on a tin can. At least it sounded that way. The aluminum in the wings of an airplane is nearly as thin as a tin can, yet strong enough to lay my heavy frame on, so that my twelve or so broken bones, including ribs, my tailbone, and several vertebrae in my neck and back, would not cut into my spinal cord. My leg was also broken. It required a tremendous presence of mind for Helen and Julie, who were also in great pain, to open the door and very gently help me onto the wing and wrap me in a tarp. I remember shaking, causing the light aluminum wing to vibrate slightly.

Was it really me lying out there that cold night on the wing of an airplane, or had I wandered off into the realms of dreams and illusion? It was a strange thought, yet it crossed my mind several times. Which would occur first, my death, Doug's death, or a new day? Or would some heroic rescuers miraculously find us before daylight and somehow get us to a hospital? Where were we, anyway? Knowing my back and ribs were probably broken and my lung damaged (I was having a very hard time breathing), I was not sure if either Doug or I would ever see daylight again. When time passed and I did not hear Doug breathe or make some noise, I feared the worst.

A dark blanket of rain clouds hid the evening stars as I came in and out of consciousness, and I may have mistaken eyes for stars as a pack of coyotes moved in. Perhaps the blood dripping from my clothes onto the sand attracted their attention. Their high-pitched howling, like a forlorn siren, penetrated the frigid night air. Hearing the howls, I called to Helen that I had heard sirens. Someone in the plane even called out, "We're over here!" Then I recognized the coyotes' cries from the numerous Scout trips of my youth.

Julie attempted to scare off the coyotes by banging together broken pieces of airplane. Soon, the dogs lost interest and wandered away. In my incoherent state, I thought, *Too bad they left. I would have liked to have grabbed a big coyote and pulled him under the tarp to keep me warm for the night.* I was so cold and in so much pain! I knew hypothermia was setting in, because I could not stop shaking. When I first gained consciousness, the pain was masked, probably because I was in shock. Now the pain became more acute, and I simply couldn't take it any longer. "Helen," I cried out, "why don't you and Julie come out here and sit me up against the plane so I can breathe?" They wisely refused. If they had tried to sit me up, with four broken vertebrae in my back and neck, I may have been paralyzed. I will be forever grateful to them for not allowing me to move one inch, despite my pleadings to the contrary.

I could hear Helen's sweet voice calling out the window offering encouragement. "Are you awake? Keep talking. Stay with me, Randy. You can't leave us. I need you!" Her great love for me transcended the walls of the aircraft.

With the awful, constant pain of a broken body, I was brought back to a stark reality—our plane had crashed in a remote, mountainous region in Arizona. The twenty-foot-high saguaro cactus looked odd with the tail of a crumpled aircraft imbedded in its lower trunk. I looked at the front of the plane—ripped off, with the motor lying on the ground—and wondered if we had really survived. No one survives an airplane crash like this! Probably due to the pain, I slipped in and out of consciousness throughout the evening and during the night.

I recall having vivid, dreamlike thoughts. Was I alive or in heaven? It didn't feel or look like I imagined heaven to be. Looking at the desert terrain, I thought, *Am I in hell? No, not that either—maybe figuratively, but not literally.* Then I came to the realization that we had actually survived a plane crash, and an overwhelming surge of gratitude came over me. I rarely cried as a youth and had not cried in decades, but I had visions of tears mixed with blood dripping off the plane into the desert sand. With this thought I prayed again, this time with more fervor. I also thought of the scripture, "The fervent prayer of a righteous man availeth much." I didn't know if I was righteous enough for my prayer to be of some avail, but I did know I could pray with all my heart. Through prayer, I came to the realization that God loves His children more than we can ever know, even more than I love my own children. Heavenly Father wants us to talk to Him often, regardless of who we are or what our circumstances are. He wants us to feel His unconditional love and his healing powers. He *will* answer our prayers.

It was wet and extremely cold (with the windchill, the temperature was in the thirties), but after my prayer I felt a surge of warmth and hope. From that moment on, my fears and worries seemed to dissipate. Somehow, I knew people would find us and get us the care we so desperately needed. Since this experience, I have often wondered why we don't take advantage of the Lord's comfort and peace every day of our lives.

CHAPTER SIX
Rescue

HELEN

Julie explained to me that a downed airplane transmits a signal from the ELT, or emergency locator transmitter. Her first thought was that we should be able to tell if the plane was giving off this signal, and she walked around the plane trying to detect a signal or light. Nothing. We had no idea the plane was indeed giving off this silent signal. All we could do was hope and pray that the FAA had heard Doug's report on the radio before we went down, and that they had notified the authorities. Our only option was to hope, pray, and wait patiently. Mercifully, the children slept part of the time, and they seemed to be all right.

The ELT's silent signal was picked up by a Southwest airliner whose flight path was several miles directly above our crash site. The signal was reported to key agencies, including the Florence County Sheriff Department, the Civil Air Patrol, and the Southern Air Rescue. To our knowledge, no GPSs (global positioning systems) were used back then, so no exact location of the crash site was given. Rescuers were given only a general area— the southeast deserts of Arizona and perhaps the valley surrounding Florence.

In Mesa, Arizona, Denny Allred, a high school teacher who volunteered for the Civil Air Patrol, was awakened in the night and informed that two families from Heber City, Utah, had crashed their plane and needed to be located. *Hmm, Heber City,* Denny thought. *These people may be LDS. Either way, we need to find them.* As Denny drove to Florence, making arrangements to help put the rescue crew together, he wondered, *I've never found survivors on any of my searches. Could this be different?* He would later tell us he had a very strong impression we were alive and needed help, so he had no time to waste. Denny loved to fly and even ran an early morning paper route so he would have extra funds for flying. This night he realized that because of the violent storm, it might be a while before he could get his fixed-wing plane up in the air.

The Southern Air Rescue Agency called one of their agents, Stuart Anderson, and sent him out to search for us in his helicopter. The storm still raged. Visibility was bad, with flying conditions at their worst. In order to search for us after dark and in hilly desert terrain, Stuart would have to fly at low altitudes. The lack of visibility gave him vertigo, forcing him to land at a nearby prison, where the bright lights helped him get his bearings.

Stuart later told me, "It was the worst vertigo I've ever experienced, and probably the worst storm I have ever flown in."

Three different times he went out—following a grid pattern—and three different times he returned to re-orient himself. His commander told him not to go out a fourth time, reminding him that his fuel was getting low and that the storm was just too dangerous. Risking his life, Stuart went out a fourth time anyway, this time using night-vision goggles and extending the grid over which he flew.

What is courage? To me, it is normal people who put their fears on hold to finish the job at hand, with no idea they are involved in a simply extraordinary act.

RANDY

I distinctly remember lying on the wing, worrying about my future status with respect to movement, since I could feel tingling sensations in my fingers and toes. Occasionally I would move my extremities, and when they moved I would think to myself, *All right . . . so far so good.*

As I wondered if anyone was trying to rescue us, I thought I heard the sounds of an aircraft. I pulled back the tarp and looked in the sky to see an aircraft flying above us at some distance, not breaking his pattern or circling back around. Julie and Helen heard it too, and they jumped out of the plane and began screaming and waving a little *Aladdin* flashlight that belonged to one of the children. It appeared their efforts were of no avail, as the aircraft was gone in seconds. We couldn't even tell if it was an airplane or helicopter.

We assumed no one on the aircraft saw us, and we were all quiet and reflective after that, not knowing what to do. But we later learned that Stuart did in fact get a glimpse of the plane as a result of the tiny flashlight. He reported his findings, and the message was relayed to Denny's crew on the ground. It is still unclear why the report Denny received was somewhat vague, with no exact coordinates—just a very general area southeast of Florence, Arizona.

Since they couldn't get their planes in the air because of the storm, Denny and the rest of the rescue crew headed out in a four-wheel-drive vehicle. They drove southeast from Florence, negotiating a maze of dirt roads in the desert. They carried units called DFs (directional finders), which give a beeping sound and display a needle that points in the direction of the ELT signal coming from a downed plane. At this point they picked up only very weak signals. It was not long before they came to a fork in the road. The crew felt that turning right and heading north was the correct direction to go. Denny later told us with some emotion (we have him on video telling about this) that a feeling entered into his heart that they should go left. It was crystal clear. He further stated, "This had nothing to do with electronics. It was a signal from high above the earth—from a loving Father in Heaven."

If they had turned right, the crew may have spent several hours—most of the night—searching in a different drainage area. There was a distinct possibility that Doug or I may not have lived to see the rescuers. But they turned left, and before long the DFs started giving a stronger signal and the needles started moving. According to Denny, the signals made a *woo woo* sound that was more satisfying to the rescue team than the sound of a fine orchestra. Denny seemed to know exactly when to stop the vehicle to get out and begin hiking.

Meanwhile, I heard a sound, opened my tarp to look out, and saw Julie standing in front of me. She said there must be people out looking for us, and she felt that taking a look around would be a good idea. "I might find lights," she said, "or something helpful out there. What do you think, Randy?"

Before I could respond to her she was gone. I thought, *Why didn't I give her good instructions—tell her to mark her path so she can get back to the plane, like in the movies when they tear off pieces of their clothes and tie them to trees?* We needed Julie, since she was the only adult that could function well and help us. We feared Helen had a broken neck and head injuries.

Anyway, Julie was gone. She later told us she walked for a while in the dark until she came to a gently sloping hill. She looked around and thought, *Are those lights? Are they coming this way?* She screamed in the direction of the lights. She was far enough away from the plane that we could not hear her.

The DF signals got louder. In fact, according to Denny, the *woo woo*s were so loud that he and the other rescuers could hardly hear each other talk. Finally, Denny said, "Turn off the DFs. I hear a lady's voice." (Later, Denny told us that at first, he heard a woman's voice in spirit only.) No doubt the crew wondered how Denny could hear anything above the noise of the storm and the directional finders, as they knew he has trouble hearing under normal conditions. When the DFs were turned off, the rescuers all heard Julie screaming at the top of the rise. Emotions ran high.

Still lying on the wing of the plane, I continued to lift my tarp and search the area. It had been nearly four hours since we had crashed. I blinked once or twice in the rain and thought I saw some lights. Soon I was sure I saw four bright blue lights, bobbing up and down, heading towards me. They were the most beautiful lights I had ever seen.

HELEN

I heard Randy calling to me that he thought someone was coming. I climbed out of the plane as quickly as my pain and physical condition would allow. Tears quickly blurred my vision of four searchlights coming toward us. Until now, I had kept my emotions in check for the benefit of Randy and the children. Now, with one giant flood of emotion, I collapsed into the first rescuer's arms, sobbing uncontrollably as he wrapped me in a blanket. When he said, "I'm Bishop Denny Allred," my heart leaped with hope. Of course, who else would the Lord send to help us but one of His servants? I've thought of that scene hundreds of times since the accident, each time with a renewed feeling of gratitude. I believe I had a small glimpse of what it will be like someday to be enfolded in the arms of Christ, and to know that final safety.

I was spent, physically and emotionally, but in a choked voice I asked Bishop Allred if he would give priesthood blessings to Randy and Doug.

One of the rescuers later told me, "When we opened the door to the plane and saw those five young children with their bright eyes, it was a sacred moment for us. We could hardly breathe for fear of disturbing the moment. You see, we have never found survivors in an airplane crash. We normally bring body bags, but for some reason, this time we brought blankets."

Stuart Anderson, the helicopter pilot, later said to a news reporter, "I am not a religious man, but God must have been their copilot." This would become the headline for the morning newspaper, *The Arizona Republic.*

I heard comments like, "There's uh—uh—nine of you, uh—all alive? Are you sure?" There was complete disbelief among the rescuers. "How did this plane get here? There is no place to land!" The rescuers were so overcome emotionally that they could hardly speak the words, "Who needs our help the most?"

While the others helped Doug and Randy, Denny did a very interesting thing. He reached into the cabin of the plane and gathered all five children around him. One of the things he said stuck with me, and I remember it as if he were uttering it today: "You have been saved this night and you have witnessed miracles. You have been saved for a purpose. You must find out what that is."

RANDY

There was a whirlwind of activity at the crash site, but one thing I remember clearly is when the EMTs told me they were going to slide me onto a hard board. I think they had already put my neck in an air brace, but I recall how carefully and gently they slid my heavy, wet body from the wing onto the board, and then set me gently on the ground. They used straps and duct tape to secure me, giving me a feeling of greater security—and feelings of gratitude for these professionals. They laid Helen alongside me, and with the duct tape we were like two mummies on the sands of Egypt. I don't recall much conversation between these two mummies, but I do recall our rescuers holding a tarp over us to keep the rain off. I was still shaking from the cold, and I checked again to make sure my fingers and toes would move. They did. *Yes!*

Most of all, I was grateful that my dear companion was alive next to me.

HELEN

The paramedics somehow got an all-terrain vehicle with medical supplies, including backboards, to the crash site. They secured Doug, Randy, and me onto boards on the soggy sand. I was close enough to Randy that I could reach over and touch his hand. He made a comment to the paramedics that was so typically Randy that I almost laughed out loud. He said, "Thank you for coming. It was so kind of you to come out here on a night like this!" I knew in a heartbeat, with great relief, that he was still the same old Randy. Meanwhile, Devon screamed hysterically as the paramedics, not knowing if he had injuries, strapped him to a board. I'm sure he was more traumatized by this than he was by the crash. It broke my heart that I could not comfort him and let him know we were safe.

The paramedics held a tarp over Randy and me to protect us from the rain. At one point, one of the medics, in a moment of distraction, let her corner drop. The accumulated water flooded down and hit me square in the face. For one brief moment I thought, *Oh, great! I survived a plane crash to be drowned by rainwater.* Because I was so tightly immobilized it took a minute to sputter a complaint. The poor paramedic was extremely flustered and apologized profusely. I wanted to say, "Are you kidding? Don't you dare apologize. You are out here in this miserable weather, saving lives and performing miracles. I couldn't be more grateful, and besides, I was thirsty anyway!" But I was too busy catching my breath to say anything.

Sometime during this flurry of activity, the large life-flight helicopters from trauma centers in Phoenix were called out, but the pilots said the weather was too severe and the terrain too rough to land at the crash site. (If the helicopters could not get there, how could a plane land there?) Somehow the paramedics would have to get us to the hospital in Florence, a small town about fifteen miles away. The life-flight helicopters would pick us up there and shuttle us to trauma centers in Phoenix. Around this time one of our heroes, Stuart Anderson, the pilot of the search helicopter, landed his chopper on a dirt road three-fourths of a mile away and hiked to the crash site. He said, "You men prepare a landing area with flares, and

I'll hike back out, get my helicopter, and bring it here. There is enough room to put one stretcher in the back, and I'll make several trips to the dirt road." There were three ambulances waiting at the dirt road to make the fifteen-mile trip to the Florence Hospital.

RANDY

Before long, I felt a tremendous wind. It was the blades of Stuart's chopper—a cold but wonderful wind. I watched it land and take off rather quickly with Doug, who was still unconscious and delirious at the time. I believe they asked a couple of the kids, including two-year-old Brittany, to get on board. Brittany announced, "I am not getting on that thing." Instead, John Schull, an EMT from the local sheriff's department, kindly carried her on his shoulders to the dirt road and put her in one of the ambulances. Over the next few weeks, John would provide us with great help and support. Months later, he and his wife and family came to Heber Valley to visit and enjoy the amenities of the area. We felt a special bond with these wonderful people.

I felt that strong wind again, and before long I was being lifted onto the chopper and flown to one of the waiting ambulances. Stuart then flew back to the crash site, where rescuers loaded Helen's stretcher on board. As the helicopter lifted off the ground, Stuart radioed his commander and said he was flying the last person out and was out of gas. *Out of gas?* Helen thought to herself. *I just crashed in an airplane, survived drowning by rain, and now we are going to run out of gas and crash in this helicopter!* They made it to the dirt road, where Stuart had to leave his chopper until he could return the next day with a gas truck.

The lights and warmth of the ambulance felt good, but I shook uncontrollably from mild hypothermia. Because of the excruciating pain I was in, I felt every bump in the dirt road. The EMTs went to work on me, inserting an IV and checking me out. At the hospital in Florence, Doug, Helen, and I were transferred to life-flight helicopters and flown to Phoenix.

Sometimes after a traumatic experience, especially when a person is in shock, he or she can have what almost feels like an out-of-body experience. I imagined myself hovering twenty feet or so above the landing pad at Scottsdale Memorial Hospital in Phoenix. For a moment, I thought I was watching the opening scene of the TV show *M*A*S*H*, where people scurry around to get the wounded into the tent hospital. It was interesting to watch my own drama, although I wished at the time that it were just a movie and not reality.

CHAPTER SEVEN
Trauma

RANDY

I was still very cold in the Scottsdale Memorial emergency room. The nurses quickly cut off all my clothes and wrapped me in warm blankets, and I finally began to warm up and stop shaking. After they gave me a shot or two for the pain, I said, "Wow, does this ever feel better!" I looked at the expressions of the doctors, nurses, and assistants to try to gauge my condition, but they were all too professional to give me any clues. They simply went to work: IVs, oxygen, heart monitor, X-rays, and direct pressure to a large gash on my head. Some of the comments I recall include "We'll need to sew that up later," "Hey, there's a break in his leg," "Let's have another X-ray of the fractures in his neck," "Careful not to move him," "Better take more pictures,"

"We'll need to order a plastic cast for the fractures in his back," "Get more oxygen—his lung is damaged," "What about these broken ribs?" and "What about his bruised heart?"

While all this was going on, I actually dosed off—or was drugged off somewhere. I came to around 6:00 AM and noticed two very impressive men in dark suits in the doorway. Later, I learned they had been waiting for three hours outside my room; they were told they could not enter the room until I was stabilized. Medical staff had informed these men that in addition to all of my broken bones, there were large bruises on my heart and lung.

I knew right away who the men were, and I announced to everyone in the room, "If you would all please take two steps back, you will get to hear these two nice Mormon elders give me a blessing of healing." The medical staff acquiesced, and there opened a nice pathway for the elders to walk through to get to me. They gingerly placed their fingers on my blood-soaked head, anointed my head with oil, and pronounced a wonderful blessing. The elder acting as voice promised that my organs would be quickly made whole and would function as intended, that my bones would heal, and that I would be blessed with competent medical help. Later, doctors could find little evidence of damage to my heart or lungs.

While I had initially mistaken them for missionaries, these men were actually high priests in the LDS Church.

President Ellsworth was the local stake president, and Bishop Walker was a local bishop. How reassuring it was to have a network of assistance and love hundreds of miles from home! I am sure both of these men had to be at work that morning, but they were willing to sacrifice a good portion of a night's sleep to serve a total stranger.

HELEN

While Julie and the children were examined at the Florence Hospital, I was flown to The Good Samaritan Trauma Center in Phoenix. After hours of X-rays, doctors informed me there were no fractures in my neck. This was, of course, an enormous relief. However, I did have a severely torn right trapezius (the large, triangular muscle extending over the back of the neck and shoulders), a concussion, a gash on my forehead that needed stitching, broken and bruised ribs, a missing tooth, and a mouthful of loose teeth.

At the crash site, when I told an EMT I could not move my right arm, he felt a large, hard bump on the back of my shoulder and said it was broken. Mysteriously, that bump disappeared. Denny Allred had given me a blessing at the crash site and had blessed me that I would be able to take care of my family. I can only imagine how much harder it would have been to take care of an active baby, a convalescing husband, and the demands of a family of eight if I had broken my shoulder.

While in the trauma center, I asked the nurse to call my brother Jim and my neighbor Chari so they could inform my family of the accident. The Associated Press had picked up the story and it was being circulated around the country, and I didn't want my children to find out about the accident from the news media.

RANDY

The night of the crash, three of Doug and Julie Wagstaff's children were at home alone: Jonathan (age eighteen), Scott (age sixteen), and Kristen (age fourteen). Around 2:00 AM, the phone rang. Jonathan heard it but ignored it at first, thinking it must be a wrong number or a prank call, as he figured no one they knew would call that time of night. The phone just kept ringing and ringing, so Jonathan finally answered. The conversation went something like this:

"Hello, is this Jonathan Wagstaff?"

"Yes."

"Is your father Doug Wagstaff?"

"Yes."

"I am sorry to inform you that your father was in a terrible airplane crash."

"How is he?"

"Well, not so good. He has serious face injuries, multiple cuts on his head, and he has lost a lot of blood.

He most likely has broken bones in his neck, back, and feet, but we are continuing to X-ray him. He is basically in critical condition, but he will survive."

"How are the others? What about everyone else?"

"We are trying to figure out what happened to the others and where they are located. Do you know a Mr. Hall?"

"Yes, of course, but this is the first I have heard of the crash."

"We do not know the status or whereabouts of any of the others. If you find any information, would you please inform us?"

To say Jonathan was stunned and shocked would be an understatement. Logically, he knew that when there is an airplane crash in a storm after dark, there are rarely any survivors. Jonathan immediately woke Scott and Kristen and told them what had happened.

The most excruciating part of this ordeal for these teenagers was not knowing the status of their mother and their other three siblings. They did not know if the rest of their family was missing, dead, or seriously injured. At this point, one of the teenagers suggested they pray together. They fell to their knees around the living room table and prayed with all their hearts, saying, among other things, "Please, Father, we need your help. Please be with our family this night and see them through this tragedy."

After the prayer, an unusual calm came over Jonathan, Scott, and Kristen, and the Spirit of God conveyed a message that their family would be all right and would survive this ordeal. Jonathan described this experience by stating, "The Spirit literally calmed us down."

After the prayer, the Wagstaff teenagers felt inspired to call their good friend and neighbor Kevin Distefano. Kevin, who was also their bishop, immediately came to their house and gave each of them a blessing. Then he got on the phone and began calling everywhere he could to find information. How comforting it must have been to have a dear friend to deal with the details and to give comfort. Once again, love manifested itself in a powerful manner when it was needed the most.

Two dreadful hours went by, and then by some miracle Bishop Distenfano located Julie at the hospital in Florence. Julie was surprised but happy to hear from her bishop, and she spoke to her three children at home, explaining that their siblings who were on the plane were doing well. Then she told them the status of their father, Doug, who was at Scottsdale Memorial Hospital in serious but stable condition.

HELEN

After I was moved to a hospital room, I had what I refer to as a "separation panic attack," which only a mother can understand. My physical pain was minor compared to the emotional trauma of feeling alone and separated from my family. I felt like I would hyperventilate with the uncertainty of not knowing how my children and husband were doing. I knew Maryann, who had been admitted to the hospital in Florence, was all alone and probably scared. Devon was somewhere in Arizona with Julie, no doubt screaming to be nursed. My daughter Jessica was all alone at college hearing the frightening news. My other three boys, ages seventeen, fifteen, and seven, were at home. I could only imagine how they were taking the news. Randy was in critical condition somewhere in a trauma center across town. My family was spread out over six locations in two states.

Once again I turned to prayer to calm my troubled heart. I knew my only source of peace at this difficult time would be a loving, understanding Heavenly Father. I poured my heart out for answers and help. It does not always happen this way, but sometimes answers to fervent prayers are immediate. Just a few minutes after closing my prayer, I received a call from the trauma center at Scottsdale Memorial Hospital. (So that's where he was!) They put Randy on the phone and he sounded well, though somewhat shaky. We spoke just a few minutes before they whisked him away for more X-rays. Then I called my boys at home. It was heart-wrenching as we cried on the phone together. At that moment, I felt incredible gratitude to be alive and able to give each other comfort. I longed to hold each of them in my arms and wipe away their tears. I was grateful for my dear friend and neighbor Chari Davis for waking my boys up at 6:30 AM and gently breaking the news to them. Love goes a long way in time of crisis, and Chari, a nurse, would be a great help on many occasions over the next few months.

Ron Stone, our stake president, lived just down the road from us in Midway. He walked to our house at 6:30 AM, met Chari, and then did something wonderful. He gave each of our three boys a blessing of comfort and assurance. President Stone has a gift for words in his normal conversation, but when directed by heavenly Beings, he spoke directly to our sons' hearts and minds. I only wish these heavenly messages could have been recorded so my sons could refer to them later in life, for the storms that always come.

As soon as I hung up, Julie called to let me know she and the children were staying at the home of John Schull, a deputy sheriff who happened to be a member of the LDS Church. Devon was doing just fine. Julie had convinced him that a bottle wasn't such a bad thing after all, especially when it contained chocolate milk. Next I received word that Jessica would be flying to Phoenix in the afternoon to be with us. What about my dear, sweet Maryann? She had been so brave and strong at the crash site. Was she really okay? I called the hospital where she was and the nurse said Maryann would be released in a few hours. They had done a CT scan of her back and would let us know the results later. She was having trouble walking and needed to use crutches. Four days later we found out she had two small fractures in her back.

Over the course of an hour, I felt the peace and calm I had prayed for, with the knowledge that all of my family members were being well cared for. I was extremely grateful for the friends, family members, and complete strangers who had come forward to make this situation so much more bearable.

Later that afternoon, Julie walked into my hospital room with Devon. I dissolved into grateful tears at the sight of my healthy, precious son. Though my injuries made it difficult to nurse him, it felt incredibly peaceful to have him in my arms again. Julie told me that Maryann and the rest of the children had been examined at the hospital in Florence. To Julie's great relief, a heart monitor on her abdomen had picked up the strong, steady, heartbeat of her unborn child. Other than a few bruises, Brittany, Brandon, and Robyn checked out fine.

Maryann was still having trouble breathing and walking, so she was admitted for the night for observation. The admitting nurse was Donna Rankin, the wife of the Chief of Police who helped lead the rescue effort. Her teenage daughter happened to be in the hospital for pneumonia, so she put Maryann in the same room so she wouldn't feel so lonely. Her daughter's name was Jessica and she had a sister named Maryann, an interesting coincidence. My Maryann received a priesthood blessing. Upon seeing this, Jessica Rankin asked for a priesthood blessing as well. Within a few hours Jessica was better and released to go home.

In the morning, Donna could tell Maryann was having a rough time. She knew Maryann was LDS, so she called a friend, who she knew was also LDS, and said, "There is a little Mormon girl in here whose parents have been in a plane crash, and she is feeling frightened and alone. I know that Mormons take care of each other, so I thought you would want to help." Within minutes the local Primary president (the leader over the children's group) arrived at the hospital, and she stayed with Maryann all afternoon.

When the hospital was ready to release Maryann, since there was no one there to take her, the Primary president, Deborah Bagnall, took her to her own home. Deborah found Maryann some clothes, and the young women from the local ward came and visited her with gifts and balloons. I was relieved and touched at how these wonderful people comforted Maryann during this difficult time.

The "Mormon Network" is an amazing thing. Over the next month, during our stay in Arizona, we had so many offers of help: houses to stay in, food, transportation, prayers, and emotional and financial support. I will be forever grateful to the Arizona Saints.

The hospital had been inundated all day by the press. Finally, hospital personnel convinced me that if I would give an interview to a member of the press, they would back off and leave us alone. During the interview, it came up that I had some premonitions that we would crash and never make it to Matzatlan. It was an interesting and irritating experience as reporters put words in my mouth and later quoted them as if I had said them. I didn't allow them to film my face as I had a missing front tooth, a bandaged forehead, and my head was at an odd angle on my shoulders. (I was worried it would frighten my children if they saw me on TV in this condition.) So, instead, the camera person filmed my twisting, wringing hands. If they gave an Academy Award for best dramatic hands, I think I would win.

That evening, whether from painkillers or thirty-six straight hours of sleeplessness, I began to doze when I saw a beautiful, blond angel at my door. It turned out to be Jessica, my eldest daughter, straight from heaven—or at least it seemed that way—come to give us comfort and encouragement. She would stay with us for the next ten days.

The next morning I was released from the hospital with a neck brace and the disheartening news that my neck would never be the same. However, I was so grateful to be alive that I wasn't at all concerned about the months of physical therapy I would need in an effort to get some movement back.

Some good friends from back home—Lee, Kathy, Doug, and Linda—drove down from Utah and picked up Jessica and me from the hospital. The nurses sneaked us out a back entrance to avoid the press. It was an overwhelming experience to feel the sunshine on my body and witness the world going on as usual. I studied a single flower growing in the hospital garden and was overcome with emotion at the beauty of it. I bent down and caressed its silken petals with tears streaming down my cheeks. It was as if I were witnessing the stunning glories of nature for the first time. My friends thought I was crying from pain and fear, but it was really out of gratitude to still be living in this beautiful world.

We drove to Scottsdale Memorial Hospital to visit Randy and Doug. Jessica and I headed to the ICU and found what the nurses told us was Randy's room. We tentatively crept into the room. We took one look at the unconscious man on the bed and walked back out again to inform the nurses they had given us the wrong room number.

"No, that is your husband!" they told me. Barely breathing and on trembling legs, I walked back into the room. It couldn't be Randy! His blond hair was dark red with dried blood. The top of his head was shaved, revealing a six-inch, jaggedly sewn gash starting at his forehead. His face was so badly swollen that his features were deformed and unfamiliar. He seemed to be hooked to every machine known to modern medicine. Jessica and I collapsed into each other's arms, fear shaking our very cores.

We made our way out of the room, concerned our sobbing would awaken Randy. The nurses in the hallway tried to appease us by telling us he had been heavily sedated and to come back when he was awake. We sat anxiously in the waiting room, afraid to voice our fears of what the future would hold.

When I met with the doctor that afternoon, I began riddling him with questions: How soon can Randy leave the hospital and get back to Utah? How soon can he start walking? Does he need surgery? The doctor shocked me into reality when he said, "Mrs. Hall, your husband is not out of the woods yet. He will probably be here for at least two to three months, and then in rehab and therapy for a year. Don't expect any miracles. He's lucky he is alive!" I thought, *Well, a miracle kept him alive, and more miracles will heal him.*

CHAPTER EIGHT
Healing

RANDY

Hospital personnel do not intentionally torture people, and they are generally wonderful caregivers, but during one X-ray, I was force-fed some thick fluid that nearly choked me. Later, during the nerve testing, a fluid (probably iodine) was injected into my spine and veins that felt like boiling water. Would the pain ever end? During one of my trips through the MRI, my arm got caught somewhere, and I announced to the technician that I thought she was breaking my arm. She panicked and then reversed the machine—no damage done to me, but the technician needed respiratory therapy.

Late in the day, I heard familiar voices outside my room in the intensive care unit. A nurse was lecturing my sweet wife and daughter Jessica about the ICU. Before I could gather my thoughts about seeing two of the most wonderful people in my life, these two lovely creatures were standing over me. All of us were choked with emotion. Helen looked so good—she was alive, whole, and real!

I asked her, "Have you always had a missing tooth?" She said, "Sure, I've always looked this goofy. I was this way when you married me. You never noticed before?" She had a gash on her forehead and moved very gingerly with bruised ribs, a torn and swollen neck, and multiple bruises, but she looked beautiful to me, like a queen in royal splendor. My eternal companion and sweetheart was at my side again and the world would be okay.

My lovely daughter Jessica looked wonderful and was there to care for me. I had no job, no health insurance, and I might not walk for a long time, but what did that matter when one was loved?

Jessica and Helen would try to hold back the tears whenever they looked directly at me, but they were not as crafty as the medical professionals, so their attempts to act nonchalant were lovingly transparent. Helen picked up my hand, the only part of me she dared touch, then kissed it and said, "Thank you for not dying." I had watched tender love scenes in great movies, but this love scene—in a stark hospital room in a faraway place—surpassed them all.

HELEN

Later in the evening when we were allowed back in Randy's room, we were amazed at how much better he looked. The swelling had gone down, his color was back, and he was much more coherent. Even the nurses and doctors were impressed at how quickly Randy was rallying. As we wondered what had caused such a marked improvement, our bishop, Brent Kelly, called from Midway and said, "Helen, I thought you would want to know that hundreds of people in the community here held a day of fasting and praying for your family." I was so moved I could hardly speak my words of gratitude.

I believe everyone has scenes that print pictures on his or her heart. When these images are recalled, they bring tears to the eyes and joy to the heart. I have one such picture in my heart's photo album. It's when I saw Maryann for the first time, two days after the crash. Julie had brought her from Florence to the hospital in Phoenix. I saw her at the end of the hallway hobbling along on her crutches. She was so pale and forlorn-looking that it broke my heart. I could hardly see through my tears to make the slow and painful trek down the hall to hold her in my arms. She was trying to be so brave, but she finally broke down and we sobbed together. My throat constricted as I tried to comfort her and tell her everything would be okay. (How could I convince her, when I wasn't convinced myself?)

She wanted to go in and see her dad, but I was afraid she would be traumatized at seeing him in his present condition. I didn't realize then how traumatized she already was. (How could I know she would suffer from post-traumatic stress disorder for many years to come?) As a young adult she would have to face her demons and work through her personal nightmare of the crash. As an eleven-year-old, however, she put on such a good show that we were all amazed at how well she seemed to be doing.

The next day, Maryann and the three young Wagstaff children flew home to Utah. It was difficult to see Maryann get on that plane and head home, but she needed to get back to school. If I had it to do over I would have kept her there with me, by my side, until I knew if she was really okay.

RANDY

I could hear a great deal of commotion outside my ICU room, and the voices sounded somewhat familiar. A nurse said, "You all can't go in there," but these men were not to be restrained. Four of our friends had come from Midway: Jim Kelson (a partner in the plane), Steve Brown, Brent Hill, and Scott Whimpey. Was I dreaming again?

They had been to the crash site and were amazed to see us but happy to administer another priesthood blessing. How wonderful to see friends from home! This visit opened the floodgates of a river of loved ones who came to comfort us, bless us, and let us know how much we were loved.

My two childhood friends Lee Sadler and Doug Harmon, with their wives Kathy and Linda, appeared one day at my bedside to cheer me up. How delightful to see familiar faces with a lifetime of shared memories. Even though it was physically painful to laugh as we reminisced about old times, the emotional healing more than compensated for the pain. Perhaps the very essence of true friendship is that all of life's experiences, both good and bad, seem to meld together, intertwining to become an enduring bond that enriches our lives.

Another friend, Tim Curtis, would make me laugh and think with him as we discussed philosophy. We went to school together in Southern California, roomed at BYU after our missions, and have always felt a special bond. He can read me like a book, and he knew all the right things to say as I lay in that hospital bed. He seemed to have a special comprehension and intuitive understanding of the miracles that had occurred, and the divine intervention that we witnessed and were continuing to experience. He helped me understand what had happened, and how it would impact me personally in the millennia to come. This gave me great peace.

Our neighbors Mark and Rae Lynne Kohler visited us and offered their parents' home in Phoenix as a place for Helen and our kids to stay and relax. So many gifts like this were freely given, with no expectations and no conditions. We cannot begin to innumerate all the many things that were done in our behalf. Our friends and loved ones seemed happy to be able to give so much to us.

In my opinion, people have an innate desire to love unconditionally, to give, and to sacrifice for others. Sometimes they just need a trigger.

HELEN

Our passage of recovery and healing was not only made easier by the loving support of people around us, but by a series of miracles that seemed to happen daily. One day Randy and I wrote down a list of all these little miracles, and the list grew to over a dozen. I remember thinking, *I wonder how many times during the daily routines of our uneventful lives, little miracles happen that we don't even notice. Do we fail to give credit to Him who makes them happen for us?* I believe that each day we awaken and greet the light and the people around us, we experience a miracle.

One of our little miracles occurred four days after the accident. Jessica, Devon, and I had stopped at the grocery store on the way from the hospital to the condo where we were staying. Because of my injuries I couldn't carry anything, so Devon and my purse were riding in the grocery cart. We finished our shopping and left the store.

About a block away I asked Jessica, "Did you get my purse out of the cart?"

She replied, "It wasn't in the cart!"

We quickly turned around, raced into the parking lot, and began our frantic search. In this purse were Jessica's and my wallets, $800 cash, credit cards, checkbooks, all our ID, an airline ticket, and a signed blank check a friend had given me.

The store employees joined our search as we scoured the inside and outside of the store, but to no avail. All the way home I was nauseated with concern over how we could possibly get by without everything in that purse. I had no other money and was feeling desperately overwhelmed when I knelt down for my nightly prayer. I felt a little sheepish as I said to the Lord, "I know you just saved all our lives, we are all healing miraculously, and you have sent many angels to help us, but I really need one more little miracle. I really need that purse!"

Two days later President Ellsworth, the man who came to the hospital early in the morning after the crash to give Randy a blessing, walked into the ICU waiting room with my purse. I was too shocked to speak. It turned out an honest man had found the purse in a parking lot around the corner from the grocery store (we have no idea how it got there). The man found President Ellsworth's business card inside and called to see if he knew how he could get this purse back to its owner. Nothing was missing—not one single thing.

Another thing that seemed like a miracle to me was when my older brother Jim came to Arizona and spent a few days with us. He said, "I couldn't stand being up in Utah. I had to come down and see what was happening for myself." He was a great comfort because he had always been like a father to me.

Ten days after the accident another miracle occurred. Members of the Church chipped in and bought airline tickets for my four children at home to fly to Phoenix to be with us for Thanksgiving. As I scanned the unloading passengers at the airport and saw my children running up to meet me, I thought my heart would burst. We all collapsed in one big hug with the reality of all we had almost lost. We later gathered in Randy's hospital room and had a family prayer of thanksgiving—another picture for my heart's photo album. I'm sure that throughout all eternity I will never forget the feelings of gratitude and love on our finest Thanksgiving Day ever.

That evening, the children and I had an exquisite Thanksgiving dinner at the Leisure World home of Jackie and Ab Winterose. Their daughter Rae Lynne Kohler (our Relief Society president in my home ward), her husband Mark, and their four daughters had come to Phoenix for the holiday. It was the first time I actually felt like eating since the accident. After dinner we sat in a huge, heated pool with a Jacuzzi. As hot water poured over my sore muscles, easing the spasms in my neck, I thought of

Randy's progress and smiled. He had been released from the ICU and put in a transitional-care unit. I watched an Arizona sun setting over an orange-and-turquoise sky silhouetted with palm trees. My children were laughing and splashing in the pool, creating another unforgettable picture. A feeling of complete contentment settled over me. I remember thinking, *Life doesn't get any better than this. I have everything that is important to me. We can survive anything together.*

CHAPTER NINE
Gratitude

RANDY

On Thanksgiving Day, when my children walked into my room, they looked so good that I felt like I was seeing them for the first time. Soon, my tall, strong boys, Jacob, Brandon, and Ryan, and my beautiful daughters, Jessica and Maryann, stood by my bedside with tear-filled eyes. I felt such a sense of gratitude that I was able to look at them as a mortal being, and I thought my heart would burst with love.

Over the years, I have found that the experience of the plane crash has changed my perspective regarding my children. I love them and I am so grateful to be in their presence that I find myself saying very little about how they should behave or live their lives. I believe my love, my example, and just living my life to the best of my ability will be the best sermon I can share with them. Occasionally, I will look for teaching moments when they come to me with questions. Anyone who knows me knows I generally have a lot to say, but my new policy of economy of voice seems to work well with my children.

One Sunday, several years after the plane crash, I was sitting in church with two of my boys. As I looked over at the boys, I thought about the plane crash and was overcome with emotion. How does one find a way to express the gratitude at just being in the presence of these growing, young souls? I know most parents have similar thoughts about their children, and yet how quickly we forget the sunlight when our kids do not perform to our expectations.

Over the next week, my brother Greg and my four sisters, Chris, Julie, Theresa, and Vita, all flew in to visit me at the hospital. Just like when I first saw my children after the plane crash, it was as if I saw my siblings for the first time. Their love made me feel whole emotionally and mentally, and they gave me hope that my broken body would soon follow.

At the time of the crash, my parents were cruising the Panama Canal. My brother and sisters opted to wait until their return to tell them what had happened. Almost two weeks after the plane crash, when my parents arrived at Salt Lake International Airport, my brother Greg and my sister

Julie sat them down and tenderly broke the news about the crash and about our injuries. My parents accepted the news quite well, although they did have a sleepless night.

The next morning, my parents flew to Phoenix and appeared in my hospital room. As I watched them enter the room, we all tried to hold back our tears. Somehow, it was as if I was a little boy with skinned knees, and my mother would make it all better. I was nearly old enough to have grandchildren myself, but now my mother sat on my bed and read history stories to me (we're both history nuts). My parents stayed in Phoenix for nearly two weeks, until I could be transferred to Salt Lake City. It is said the greatest love is that of a mother for her child. Is it because mothers give more, sacrifice more, and thus love more? Someone once said that we love a person for what we do for him or her, not vice versa. Love is defined many ways, but I believe that without the concept of giving and sacrifice at the very core, any definition would be incomplete.

HELEN

It was an unsettling emotion to watch my best friend, lover, confidant, provider, and the father of my children lay incapacitated in a hospital bed. Would he ever be able to fully function again?

Though it was a worrisome time for me it was also a very sacred time. I often reflect on that time with fond memories. As the three of us—Randy, Devon, and I—hung out in the hospital together, we learned some very important lessons. Our priorities became crystal clear as our beliefs and love of family were eternally solidified. It was a great gift for us to spend long, quiet hours together. Sometimes we watched old movies and cried in parts that had never affected us before. We had seen the original version of *The Parent Trap* many times in the past and never been emotionally moved like we were watching it in that hospital room. We looked at each other with tears streaming down our faces and then, feeling silly, broke out laughing.

Devon snuggled up next to Randy on the hospital bed and took his naps. When he was awake Devon perched on top of Randy's large, plastic body brace. It resembled a turtle shell and made Devon giggle as he straddled it like a ride-on toy. When he was bored with that, he would grab Randy's catheter hose and watch Daddy yelp. He would sometimes get frustrated that his previously playful daddy would not get down on the floor and romp with him.

There was an epidemic of RSV at the time, so the nurses insisted that Devon stay in Randy's sterilized room. This was where Devon learned to crawl. The scene of him crawling on that white, shiny floor and pulling himself up on the chrome bedrail is another picture I'll never forget.

We learned to appreciate each little step Randy took in regaining his health. While Devon was learning to crawl, his forty-five-year-old father was learning to walk again. After Randy got out of the ICU, the physical therapists put him on a "slant board," a board on a hydraulic lift that gradually tilted him from a prone position to an upright position. The first attempt failed, and Randy passed out before he was halfway up. Each day they raised his head a little higher before he was overcome with dizziness.

I will never forget, more than two weeks after the accident, when the therapists finally got Randy on his feet for the first time. It took two strong men to drag him, with the help of a therapy belt and a walker, to a standing position. I was grateful I was behind Randy so he could not see the tears streaming down my face. I am not sure if I was crying from relief at the accomplishment or from fear at seeing how laborious and painful it was for him. I was terrified he might never walk alone again. He could go only a few feet before he started to pass out with the pain.

I was continually amazed at Randy's positive attitude. He would get so excited at each little improvement. The nurses and doctors often commented on how upbeat Randy was, and they claimed that was why he was healing so quickly. They would make comments like, "There are patients in this hospital that don't have anywhere near the injuries that Randy has, and he will be released sooner than they will." The doctors also said Randy was the type of patient that made their jobs worthwhile.

We concluded that the severity and duration of an injury is directly proportional to one's attitude and determination to heal. That, in turn, is directly influenced by one's faith in a divine power to assist in healing. The prayers and fasting of so many, and the faith-generated priesthood blessings Randy received, had a major impact on his healing, both physically and emotionally. It makes me wonder if every hospital should have a doctor whose only task is to encourage positive attitudes and promote faith in the healing power from God.

RANDY

Out of intensive care for nearly a week, I could partially sit up for a minute or two without substantial pain, or even ride in a wheelchair for a minute or so. This afforded me the opportunity of going on a journey to the bathroom, which was about eight feet from my bed, for an attempt to urinate for the first time in nearly three weeks without the aid of a tube. Yes, the dreaded catheter had been yanked out, and after scraping me off the ceiling, my nice nurse said it would stay out if my eight-foot trek to the great white throne was successful.

Had I not climbed the great Half Dome in Yosemite, California, with my daughter, Jessica? Upon reaching the summit we lay on a knife-edge cliff and looked down 6,000 feet at the ant-like people in Yosemite Valley below, feeling like we had conquered Everest. Fear was not in the Hall lexicon. Or was it? Surely I could make this new journey.

I had only known fear a few times in my life. Three weeks earlier during the plane crash, I had gained much insight regarding my fears, but I never expected to experience fear so soon again, especially in a place as common as a restroom. The nurse helped me get there, and then left me. There I sat, all alone on the "throne" in complete terror, trying to get my bladder muscles to cooperate and relax.

Knowing the catheter would have to be re-inserted if I were not successful was frightening, but even greater was the fear of passing out, falling, and re-injuring myself. My broken bones were not cooperating and I could not seem to hold myself up. I called for my nurse. She did not hear me. I knocked on the door, but to no avail. I was fading fast, and all I could see were blackness and stars. Finally, the door opened and the nurse asked, "Are you finished?" "Please . . . help . . . me," I mumbled. "I failed the only assignment you have given me today." As she helped me back in bed, I awaited the dreaded catheter. I thought of the look on Princess Leia's face in *Star Wars* when Darth Vader brings in the torture machine with that awful-looking needle.

While waiting for the nurse to do her work, I thought about fear again. Is fear mostly a perception? I remember my friend Lee walking on the rail above Hoover Dam with no fear. I tried it too, but looking down eight hundred feet gave me such an eerie, uncomfortable feeling that I opted to walk on the sidewalk. Had I not looked down I would have been fine. Obviously, a certain amount of fear is good because it keeps us alert and helps us avoid danger—the adrenaline flows to protect us. Yet too much fear can be debilitating.

In the 1970s, the Intermountain Collegiate Downhill Ski Race was held at Snow Basin, Utah, and I participated with the BYU ski team. Most people have never skied Snow Basin, so they may not consider the Snow Basin Downhill anything special. Since it was the venue for the 2002 Olympic downhill, however, many people have taken a second look. Some Olympic skiers hit ninety miles per hour at this venue. Racers in the 1970s ran a slightly different course, reaching speeds of seventy-five to eighty miles per hour.

After taking two lifts up the mountain, we continued hiking a ridge to the top of a sixty-degree "snow chute," a virtual cliff that had avalanched the day before our race. Normally, for a downhill race, a skier can look down the hill and see most of the gates or poles, but standing at the top of these pinnacles, I could only see the first two gates; after that, the course disappeared over the cliff. It was great for acceleration to eighty miles per hour, but not good for the weak of heart. Then came a fall-away jumper, requiring a premeditated pre-jump to avoid too much airtime, and then the skier would enter the canyon at top speed. The key to skiing in the canyon was avoiding trees, rocks, hay bales, and spectators.

You could experience some of the sensation of a downhill ski race by driving your car off the highway at eighty miles per hour onto bumpy terrain in desert or canyon country. (I do not recommend this; it's the thought that counts.) You would maybe feel how a downhill racer's legs act like shock absorbers, recoiling one or two times per second while he is trying to carve precise, knife-like turns with his skis' metal edges. He fights all the way down the mountain to keep his line and to stay on course by setting his skis at more than a forty-five-degree angle at times, hoping those metal edges hold on to the snow and ice so he can stay on course.

If there is some ballerina-like poise and grace in the slalom race (my favorite), then the downhill race is more like a ragtag, desert motorcycle race. The skier must think two or three gates ahead and consider every change in terrain on the course. One becomes hyper-alert. I like the way a rock-climbing friend described his experience on a major climb: "I never felt so alive as when I took life to the very edge."

Rock climbing and downhill racing have much in common. The adrenaline rush is addicting. Upon crossing the finish line and gliding fifty yards to a stop, the feeling

117

was so exhilarating that I had crazy thoughts like, "I'm ready to go again. I think I can do it a little faster next time."

Fear is an emotional response that can trigger physical reactions, such as relaxing certain muscles that control the bladder. There were no outhouses at Snow Basin at 11,000 feet. Clouds began to form below us and visibility dropped to 200 to 300 yards, yet officials kept sending racers down the course, and my anxiety and fear increased. Soon, I was wishing for an outhouse. We visited nearby trees to relieve ourselves that scary morning, but of course macho racers would never admit to any fear on the mountain. However, when my teammate Scott crashed, broke some ribs, ruptured his kidney, and was in the hospital for six weeks, and a fellow racer from the University of Utah was killed when he skied into a tree the next year, we finally owned up to our fears.

So, I lay on the hospital bed thinking how my fear at the top of a racecourse caused me to urinate, yet my fear in the hospital would not allow me to do so. While this may not be one of life's great paradoxes, it did seem ironic.

This time when the nurse inserted the evil catheter, I tried something new: the relaxing and breathing techniques Helen and I were taught prior to "natural" childbirth. (Of course, Helen was the birther; I was just the heavy breather and coach.) I not only relaxed, but I fortified myself by having a little pep talk, telling myself I could indeed handle this pain. *In fact,* I insisted to myself, *I can handle more, so bring it on.* In other words, I changed my perception and the fear subsided.

I believe if we prepare and fortify ourselves, we can summon our courage and handle almost anything life throws at us. If we trust our inner self in times of peril, we can surprise ourselves by performing at a higher level than we would have ever dreamed possible. I am still amazed at the courage everyone in the plane exhibited during our ordeal. They inspired me to rise to a higher level of performance.

Shakespeare says it well in *Henry VIII:*

In peace, there's nothing that becomes a man
As modest stillness and humility.
But when the blast of war blows in our ears,
Then imitate the action of the tiger:
Stiffen the sinews, summon up the blood,
Disguise fair Nature with hard-favored rage . . .
Now set the teeth and stretch the nostril wide,
Hold hard the breath, and bend up every spirit
To his full height.

CHAPTER TEN
Home

HELEN

On our last Sunday in Arizona, I found a local LDS chapel and attended sacrament meeting. I was looking for a little solace, as I had been very discouraged and worried about our situation. The aviation insurance on Doug's plane should have covered our hospital bills, but the company was refusing to pay, due to some technicality. Our hospital bills were well over $100,000 and still climbing. Randy wouldn't be able to work for an indefinite period of time. I would not be able to work, as I would need to be his full-time nurse. He and I were still in a great deal of physical pain. Our savings were gone with the loss of our business. In short, the future looked pretty frightening.

I found the comfort I needed from the hymn we sang that Sunday in sacrament meeting, "Where Can I Turn for Peace?"

Where, when my aching grows
Where, when I languish,
Where, in my need to know, where can I run?
Where is the quiet hand to calm my anguish?
Who, who can understand?
He, only One.

He answers privately,
Reaches my reaching
In my Gethsemane, Savior and Friend.
Gentle the peace he finds for my beseeching.
Constant He is and kind,
 Love without end.
("Where Can I Turn for Peace?", *Hymns,* no. 129)

I began to understand that adversity has the potential to either exalt us or destroy us. When we are going through an extremely difficult experience, it is almost impossible to stay in a positive mode. But if we can scrape together just one seed of faith, we might realize that if we can just get on down the road, someday we will be able to look back and understand the reasons for the trial. The baggage of pain can weigh us down and wear us out, or we can turn our pain over to the Lord and be encircled in His healing arms. We can become embittered or enlightened. It is our choice.

Before Randy was released from the hospital, I felt a compelling need to visit the crash site. So, on a warm, sunny afternoon, Denny Allred (the team leader for the rescue effort) took Randy's parents, Devon, and me fifteen miles past Florence on a dirt road. As we drove, Denny recounted the events of that night that had made our rescue possible. He told how every previous time he had been called out on a search-and-rescue mission he had gone out in a fixed-wing airplane, not a four-wheel-drive vehicle. Because the weather was so bad the night of our crash, it wasn't safe to go in a plane. He reminded us how, as the search party drove toward Florence, he felt inspired as to the roads and direction they should take. He said they were inspired as to when they should stop the vehicle and start hiking. It was pitch-black in a bad rainstorm, and yet they were directed where to go.

We stopped the car and began the three-quarter-mile hike to the crash site. Denny carried Devon, now seven months old. I was surprised that he so willingly went to Denny, since he had always been a mama's boy and would normally freak out if someone else tried to hold him. He must have sensed what Denny meant to our family.

My heart began racing and I was dizzy with fear of the flashbacks that might come. I hoped that coming to this place on a bright, sunny day would abate the feelings of terror lingering from that cold, stormy night. What it really did was reaffirm in my mind the miracle that had taken place. I stood gaping at the huge cacti, gullies, ravines, and unforgiving, harsh surroundings. We found the top of the saguaro cactus the plane had lopped off, the large craters the bouncing plane had created, and the final resting place where two frightened families spent three and a half hours anxiously awaiting their fate. Now, on our visit to the site, we dropped to our knees and I gave a prayer of thanksgiving for the miracle that had taken place there. The words that tumbled out of my mouth surprised me, and they would only make sense to me when I recalled them a month later. I closed my eyes as I breathed deeply of the pungent, warm desert air. As my tears flowed freely I remembered the tears that mingled with rain on this same sand three long weeks before.

Twenty-seven days after that fateful night, on December 11, Randy was released from Scottsdale Memorial Hospital. We were going home! He still could not sit up for more than a few minutes at a time due to the extreme pain in his back, so he had to ride in an ambulance to the airport and then be loaded onto a gurney and onto a commercial plane. Because of strict FAA regulations, we dreaded the "your seats must remain in the upright position during takeoff" announcement over the intercom. I was sure Randy would pass out from pain before the flight attendant allowed us to recline his seat. The thrill of going home barely overrode the fear of flying again. For the next two hours, until we touched down at the Salt Lake airport, I would vacillate between excitement and nauseated panic. I planned to use the "barf bag" in the seat pocket to prevent hyperventilation. During the flight, a couple next to us asked us what had happened to Randy. When we told them we had been in a plane crash, their eyes went wide, and for the rest of the flight they seemed as nervous as we were. (I'm sure they thought we were bad luck.)

By the time we landed, Randy was chalk-white with pain. On the way out we told the pilot he did a fine job landing, much better than our last one.

As we rolled Randy off the plane on a gurney and into the terminal, we caught sight of the crowd of people who had come to meet us. Neighbors, friends, and extended family were lined up, but the thing that dissolved my resolve not to cry was when I saw my aging mother in her wheelchair. Clearly, she had made a great effort to be there in her frail condition. As I greeted those I hold most dear, I wondered if this was what it would be like to get to heaven and reunite with our loved ones. I don't remember ever feeling happier than at that moment.

We took the one-hour ride from Salt Lake to Midway in an ambulance. As we crested the highway coming from Park City and down into Midway, I got a glimpse of the breathtaking valley we call home. I was so overcome with emotion that the ambulance driver started to panic, thinking something had just happened to Randy. He didn't understand that my tears were grateful tears of joy at the prospect of finally being home.

It was fourteen days until Christmas. The children had bought a Christmas tree and dragged the decorations out of the storage shed. They had decorated the whole house inside and out. The Christmas spirit permeated every inch of our home.

RANDY

The first thing I noticed in the house was the beautiful Christmas tree and all the Christmas decorations. Had Helen somehow sneaked home and done this? No, it was our boys and their friends, along with other helpers. They had dug everything out and meticulously decorated the house just the way Helen would have done it, using many of her handcrafted decorations. The boys had smirks on their faces, which made it all the more fun to see them.

The high priests in my quorum, mostly older men, had obtained a hospital bed from a local storage building. It was extremely heavy, but they were able to muscle it into our family room and set up a makeshift hospital room for me. Once again the floodgates opened, and many neighbors and friends in the community visited and brought food, goodies, money, and lots of cheer. While we were so grateful for the many acts of kindness, we began to feel a little guilty about the attention and all the sacrifices made in our behalf. We felt people were doing too much and that it was not fair for us to receive so much, including the financial donations. We would say, "We're fine. Please go about your business. We're doing okay. We are past the worst part, and we'll be fine. Please, no more food, no money, no help."

It was at this time that I expressed my concerns to a friend and neighbor, Norm Kohler. We had worked in Scouting together, and we felt a special bond.

Norm knew me well enough to be upfront with me, and he said something along these lines: "Whoa there, partner. You need to sit back, relax, and concentrate on healing. It is your time to receive from your friends and loved ones, and to not worry about it. We're not doing this out of any obligation or assignment. We're doing this because we really want to do it. We enjoy it, and it is what makes us happy. There is nothing we would rather do. You just need to learn to be a good receiver right now. It is your turn. There will come a time when you will be whole again, and in turn you can do likewise for someone else. You will become a giver again—your time will come. It is called the cycle of life." Wow, what a revelation! I smiled and said, "We'll try."

There is one more person I tried to slow down with no success—the one who became my personal nurse and who had always been my aid, my confidant, my sounding board, and my sweetheart. For several months after the crash, Helen took care of my every need, some of which were not so pleasant. She would even drive me to feed the ducks in Snake Creek Canyon. Sometimes she would look at me and say, "Oh, you are getting that 'feed the ducks' look on your face again," but she would never complain, never protest, never grumble. I would say to her, "Look, honung [that's Swedish for honey, although the Swedes never use it as a term of endearment; it would sound more like calling someone "syrup"], you need to get out more, go for a drive, go to the library, go visit some friends, go shopping. Better yet go skiing, if your neck will take it." What would she say? "Honung, you need my help. I'm not leaving you. Now let me tell you something. I'm not doing this for any other reason other than I want to. I'm okay with it. I love you. This is where I want to be, and this is what I want to do. Now suck it up, enjoy it, and stop fussing over me and the other people helping us, and get on with your healing."

I had tried in my life to imagine what angels would sound like, but my quest was over, for Helen's voice was the sweet voice of an angel.

CHAPTER ELEVEN
Enduring

HELEN

Our first Sunday home in Midway, I attended church. I had been feeling rather discouraged and needed the lift a Church service could give me. The opening song was "I Know That My Redeemer Lives." It was as if the Tabernacle Choir was singing it. The lyrics had never before filled my heart so profoundly as they did that morning.

I know that my Redeemer lives.
What comfort this sweet sentence gives! . . .
He lives to bless me with his love.
He lives to plead for me above.
He lives my hungry soul to feed.
He lives to bless in time of need. . . .

He lives to comfort me when faint.
He lives to hear my soul's complaint.
He lives to silence all my fears.
He lives to wipe away my tears.
He lives to calm my troubled heart.
He lives all blessings to impart. . . .

He lives! All glory to his name!
He lives, my Savior, still the same.
Oh, sweet the joy this sentence gives:
I know that my Redeemer lives!

("I Know That My Redeemer Lives," *Hymns,* No. 136)

By the time the song was over, tears streamed down my face, and I knew my Heavenly Father loved me and was aware of my needs.

Randy's cheerful attitude continued while he was convalescing. I'm sure that is why he healed so much more quickly than the doctors expected. His patience and determination kept me from going into the depths of despair. I was going to physical therapy for my neck, but the progress was slow and the headaches almost unbearable. The demands of taking care of my family and home in this condition were overwhelming. It was a major, twenty-minute undertaking just to get Randy up on his walker and into the bathroom. He needed to be fed and bathed, and he needed to be watched over all day. The children all pitched in, and because we were all so grateful he was alive, we considered it a privilege to wait on him.

One day, when I was feeling a little sorry for myself, I ran into a friend at the supermarket whose husband was dying from Lou Gehrig's disease. The overwhelming nature of her burden became so clear that I immediately burst into tears. She had been the main caregiver for her bedridden husband for several years, but at least I had the consolation that my husband would get better. Her husband's disease would soon take his life. As I hugged her and told her I now understood what she was going through, gratitude for my own situation returned. I was humbled and amazed that she was able to do all she had done.

Our children had not asked for anything for Christmas and were not expecting any gifts, but during December, presents mysteriously appeared under our tree. Many friends and family members made sacrifices on behalf of our family. Every year my sister-in-law's family would exchange gifts with each other. This year they decided to forgo the gift exchange and pool the money they would have spent and give it to our family. It was a sizable check that helped defer some of our medical expenses. They gave it freely and experienced the true meaning of Christmas.

A week before Christmas, a saintly lady from our ward came by with a plate of goodies. You know the type; she has a scripture memorized for every occasion. We keep thinking she is going to be instantly translated just like the city of Enoch in the Bible. She began talking and there they were: the exact words I had used in my prayer the sunny day I revisited the crash site. I was speechless. Then I realized she was reciting a scripture from the Book of Mormon. I asked her which one it was and of course she knew the exact reference—Mosiah 24:14. It reads, "And I will also ease the burdens which are put upon your shoulders . . . and this will I do that ye may stand as witnesses for me hereafter, and that ye may know of a surety that I, the Lord God, do visit my people in their afflictions." It occurred to me that I needed to stand as a witness and that I had committed to do so in my prayer on the desert sand. What better time than during the Christmas season to witness of our Savior's love.

It turned out to be, in every way, our best Christmas. All of a sudden the usual craziness and hoopla of the holiday season seemed trivial and unimportant. I think it was the first Christmas I truly understood the love the Christ child brought to the world when He was born. I will always treasure the tangible spirit of love we felt during our most memorable and remarkable holiday season.

On Christmas Eve, Randy had his first social outing since the accident. We painstakingly got him into the car and took him to the annual Hall family Christmas dinner and program at his parents' house just two miles away.

(This tradition started with Randy's great grandparents.) It was a very emotional evening as we shared some special memories and our feelings of gratitude for the Savior, whose birth we were celebrating.

The next day, all six of my brothers and sisters, my mother, and over thirty nieces and nephews gathered in a Christmas celebration at our home. After dinner we visited and talked of the many miracles that had allowed us to be together on this sacred day.

A few weeks after Christmas, a very special friend, Diane, came to our door with a warm loaf of homemade bread. I invited her in for a visit. She, her husband, and their seven children lived in a humble, one-bedroom cabin with a loft. The cabin belonged to her father. For years they had been trying to save the down payment to purchase a home of their own.

As she was leaving she handed me an envelope. I opened it shortly after she left and was astounded to find a check for $1,000. I sat on the couch and cried at the humble, sweet generosity of this dear family. Later I called her and, choked with emotion, told her we would keep the check so we could put it in our scrapbook as a reminder of unconditional, pure, Christlike love. We would never cash it, as it was worth more to us than its monetary value. We were blessed by so many acts of kindness and innumerable deeds of love.

RANDY

Convalescing is difficult at best for an active person. I kept thinking I must do something productive. Lying in bed during the day is not something I had ever dreamed of. I felt I should be doing something all the time, yet people kept telling me I needed to focus on healing. How does one do that? *Okay, body, heal thyself! Come on, you big oaf, I'm waiting! Hey, pain, cease this minute! Okay, I am giving you twenty-four hours to heal, or else!* It is amazing the thoughts one has while lying in bed all day.

I tried not to allow myself to worry about our financial situation. What could I do for work to support my family, and how could we ever get out from under our debt? Should I teach at the local community college? Let's see, the starting salary would be about $28,000 per year. That would pay most of our bills, but then what? I graduated with a degree in education and have wanted to teach my whole life, but business interests kept pulling me away. Perhaps being one of the founders of a successful company and having thirty years of business experience would allow me to share some personal expertise with students within the context of more current marketing and management strategies. Perhaps I could even write a book on marketing in the food industry to use as a text.

With six kids to raise, send through college, support on missions, etc., I would most likely need a part-time business on the side to subsidize an entry-level teaching job. I started to envision various small enterprises I could do on the side while teaching. From my hospital bed, I researched a number of small businesses, including the telecommunications business, namely long distance and pay phones, and started to formalize a business plan. If nothing else it helped take my mind off the convalescing process. (Later, as a part-time job, I would buy pay phones and sell long-distance access to businesses.)

It was during my time of serious reflection and mixed emotions that Captain, our golden retriever, would lie by my bedside and look up at me with those deep, empathetic eyes. I would consult with him about my problems and my concern for the future of my family. He would wag his tail a little and gaze more intently at me, as if he somehow understood my dilemma and concerns, and then look at me as if to say, "Everything will be okay, so relax, kid."

Captain gave me great comfort at this time, as he had done for so many years with our family. He had definitely been part of the glue that held our family together during trying times. A dog does not judge, weigh, or measure people. He is incapable of malice, and is quick to forget and forgive. I could yell at Captain and threaten him with his life for urinating on the neighbor's woodpile, and minutes later he would forget I had been mad at him. Dogs are great listeners, and they seem to always be interested in the things you are interested in, especially anything having to do with the smell of food or being outdoors. With a little piece of meat one can get a dog to do almost anything and follow almost anywhere. Canines seem so content with their existence.

At this time I was extremely envious of Captain, wishing my life was as simple as his. He would lie there so peacefully, with absolutely nothing to stress about. All he needed was a little food, a nice place to nap, a pat on the head once in a while, and a chance to romp outside from time to time. Why couldn't my needs be so simple? Maybe dogs have an innate ability to live totally in the moment, and in this realm they find great pleasure.

Captain has had some challenging moments, like the time he chased a porcupine into a hole and came out with quills all over his face, in his mouth, and down his throat. Clearly in excruciating pain, he yelped until the vet could put him to sleep and pull out the quills.

Then there was the time Captain chased a pickup truck full of teenagers. Most cars would not merit his attention; only loud trucks and interesting tractors and the like would rise to the level of something worthy of a good chase. This day, with the teenagers provoking him, he got caught under the wheels of their truck. They simply drove off, leaving him lying in the middle of the street. When Maryann came out and found him, his midsection and hind legs were paralyzed and flattened. Our children assumed many bones were broken, but I suggested we pump him back up with air. That went over like a cheerleader at a funeral. Captain spent the weekend at the vet, and the next week he was running around, probably wondering what everyone was worried about. Time to romp, eat, and sleep again. Adversity, setbacks, and challenges in a dog's life are soon forgotten, and then the present joy is once again the essence of his life.

Our family experienced over a dozen such traumatic events—events that were dramatic for us but quickly forgotten by Captain. After living with us for fifteen years, this wonderful companion and mentor moved on to another life filled with adventure and love. After his passing, Helen wrote his life story as a Christmas present for the children.

While I may not be quite as content as Captain, since the accident I have realized that my life is good—very good. I have an extraordinary companion by my side, six awesome kids, two great parents that are alive and healthy, wonderful friends and neighbors, and I live in a beautiful place in a nice, warm home. I am not sure I could ask much more from life.

The plane crash has helped Helen and me realize that each day, each hour, each moment that we live is truly a gift from Heaven. It has been years since the crash, yet not a day goes by that we do not take time to reflect on the gift of that day and the value of each moment. There is so much to glean from the present. I believe the ability to live in the present is something that requires daily practice, and we are working on it.

There are two words in Swedish, *atnjuta* and *trivas*, which do not translate into English very well. During the Winter Olympics, Soldier Hollow here in Midway hosted the Nordic events. We had families of Swedish and Norwegian athletes staying in our home and in my parents' home. I asked them many times if they could come up with English words for these two words, and without fail, they could not translate these words to my satisfaction or their own satisfaction. The closest I can come for *atnjuta* is to find enjoyment, relish, feel, savor, or take pleasure in. The word *trivas* means to feel comfortable, even to thrive, to flourish, to like, to feel at home, to be comfortable in your own skin where you are in your life. These two words help inspire me to live in the present.

Because I now realize that dwelling on the past takes away from present joy, I find myself quoting an unknown author: "Yesterday is history, tomorrow is a mystery, today is a gift. That is why it is called the present."

I believe most humans are on a quest for happiness. The Prophet Joseph Smith said, "Happiness is the object and design of our existence" (Joseph Smith, B.H. Roberts, *History of the Church of Jesus Christ of Latter-day Saints,* 5:134). I believe happiness is not found in the past or in the future, but by finding as much peace, love, and joy as possible in the present.

CHAPTER TWELVE
Refining

HELEN

During our recovery I had the distinct impression the plane crash would not be the most difficult experience we would go through in this life. I wondered if this refiner's fire was meant to forge us into something stronger so we could face even more difficult challenges. My feelings were correct. Since the plane crash, we have had trials that were much more difficult.

The September after the plane crash, my daughter Jessica was involved in a rollover accident. She left the house at 6:00 in the morning to go to her job in Park City. As she rounded a corner on a curvy country road, a low tire caused her car to spin out of control, and it rolled several times down a steep, 100-foot embankment. No one saw the accident, and the car was not visible to passing motorists. One hour after Jessica left our house, someone from her place of employment called and asked where she was. "She is not there?" I said anxiously. "She should have been there half an hour ago."

With trepidation I walked out onto our front porch and looked northward. The sky was filled with smoke from recent forest fires, so I thought maybe the highway to Park City had been closed. Worried about my oldest child, I jumped when the phone rang again a few minutes later. A man at the scene of the accident was calling from his cell phone.

"Your daughter has been in a serious accident on River Road," he said.

"How serious?" I asked.

"You better get over here," he replied solemnly. "An ambulance has been called."

Randy and I jumped in the car and raced to the scene. Since River Road is only five minutes away, I realized that in the hour since Jessica had left home, the ambulance had time to come, pick her up, and get her to the hospital. Therefore, when we arrived at the scene and I saw a mangled mass of blue metal a hundred feet below the road and a body covered up with a tarp seventy feet from the wreckage, my worst fears were confirmed. People were standing by her, but not working on her. My mind raced. There was no ambulance; they must have sent it home and called the coroner.

I heard someone screaming hysterically as I got out of the car and stumbled down the embankment. I've heard the phrase *weak in the knees* but never understood it until that moment. Suddenly, I realized the person screaming was me. As I collapsed at the side of the road, I heard a fragile but stern little voice, "Mom! Calm down! I'm okay!" Jessica had pulled the cover off her head to see who was screaming.

It turned out she was cold after lying in the icy, wet pasture, and someone had put a blanket over her. Jessica had covered her head to get warm faster. After she crashed she could smell gas so she had dragged herself out of the back of her demolished car. She pulled her broken body with her one good arm seventy feet in hopes someone driving by would see her. She later told us she prayed her little heart out that someone would stop and help her.

A friend of ours, John Probst, had driven by and heard a voice say, "There's been an accident. Turn around and go back." He was startled and looked in the back seat to see who was talking. He turned his car around, went back, and still not seeing anything, stopped and got out. Then he saw Jessica down in the field.

The ambulance arrived shortly after we did. Jessica spent almost three weeks in the hospital. She had a broken pelvis, a broken shoulder, several broken ribs, a separated SI joint, and internal bleeding. She had to endure a very risky and painful operation to pin her SI joint back together.

The evening after the operation I was driving home from the hospital and wondered why Jessica had to go through this. My heart ached for her and I was pretty discouraged. A song came over the radio that I was familiar with but had never heard played on a public station. I was convinced that it was the song I needed to hear and that it was playing just for me. The words from Janice Kapp Perry's song "The Test" settled in my soul:

From the depths of sorrow I cry.
Though pains of grief within my soul arise
The whisp'rings of the Spirit still my cries:
Didn't He say He sent us to be tested?
Didn't He say the way would not be sure?
But didn't He say we could live with Him forevermore,
Well and whole, if we but patiently endure?
After the trial we will be blessed,
But this life is the test.

Jessica was definitely being tested. She would spend almost five months on a walker and using crutches. It was a difficult time for the family, but once again we were grateful for the gift of life.

The refiner's fire continued to burn in our lives after the plane crash. Life is a continuous learning process, and we had much to learn. The saying "What doesn't kill you will only make you stronger" was quickly becoming a family motto I wasn't sure I wanted. In the next few years we would experience many more "growing experiences."

We had several skiing accidents, ranging from Randy's shattered leg to Jacob's broken neck. Another serious car accident resulted in our son-in-law Shane's broken neck. My mother, father, grandmother, and brother passed away in less than three years. I came down with fibromyalgia. Maryann witnessed a suicide and suffered from severe depression of which we were unaware. A few years later she was in Guatemala giving of her time volunteering in an orphanage and at schools. One day on a hike with friends, she was brutally attacked at gunpoint. It took her years to recuperate emotionally from the attack.

This was the trial that was particularly difficult for me, and I found it close to impossible to not be bitter and angry. Giving it over to God finally brought both Maryann and our family the peace we needed. Her attackers were later captured and executed. They had killed a tourist, so we believe Maryann was protected and spared for a reason.

Through all of these challenges we were also experiencing major financial problems. We often found ourselves going into survival mode with the one constant thread that helped us endure and understand—the love of our Savior. God does not inflict pain upon us; rather, He sustains us through our pain.

I believe that sometimes the Lord chooses to influence events in a way that will miraculously change the outcome. I am not sure why He sometimes intervenes to perform His miracles, but other times seems to steps back and let us experience heart-wrenching and difficult trials. However, I am sure of this: In His infinite wisdom, God knows the individual life plans that will bring us the most growth and help us secure an unwavering knowledge of His Son's Atonement.

Divine intervention, which reveals the hand of God, can happen in our lives if it is in accordance with our individual plan of salvation. As we pray for miracles, God will either touch our lives by granting those miracles, or He will sustain us through our toughest ordeals. It then becomes our responsibility to bear witness of His perfect love, mercy, and goodness.

I don't know what the future holds, but I understand that whatever challenges may come, God will carry us through. And, when all is said and done, I'll rest assured knowing I am infinitely grateful for the privilege of life and the gift of love.

Several years after the crash, I was cleaning and came across a small, yellowed box my mother had given me years earlier. In awe, I sat on my bed and gently opened it and took out the fragile, almost sacred contents. There was a letter my grandmother had written when she was just seven to her beloved sister.

As I traced the letters she had meticulously made with her small hands, tears clouded my eyes. I still missed her after all these many years. I was thirteen when she succumbed to cancer, and I still remember the overwhelming sense of loss when she died. Right before closing her casket, my mother, the oldest of my grandmother's eight children, removed her mother's wedding ring. My grandmother had asked my mother to give the ring to me when she died. Since my fingers were too small, I wore the ring for many years on a gold chain around my neck. It was a constant reminder that my grandmother was in heaven looking out for me. When I was tempted to make a bad decision, I would think of her. I never wanted to do anything to disappoint her, for she was a saint if there ever was one.

The last item in the box was a small, delicate envelope. I held my breath as I opened it and pulled out the small, ribbon-bound lock of my grandmother's hair from when she was eight years old. As I gently twirled the lock of hair in my fingers, I involuntarily spoke out loud the words, "It was you."

It wasn't a question but a statement. I knew at that moment that it was my grandmother who had been there with us in the plane crash. She was the angel that God had sent to protect six-month-old Devon as he flew through the cabin. I felt it with every fiber of my being and sat on the bed sobbing in gratitude that she had been there.

I thought of the other times I had felt my grandmother's presence after her passing. I felt the presence of spirits of my loved ones on my wedding day, as if they were confirming my choice of a husband. I believe at the birth of each of our children my grandmother was there, bringing to earth each new little spirit as he or she began this grand mortal experience. And I am certain she was nearby, along with other appointed angels, to see us through all the refining experiences our family would face.

I am convinced my deceased grandmother would talk to Devon when he was a baby. From the time he was only a few months old, when anyone would talk to him his little face would light up and he would jabber and squeal. Sometimes he would do this when no one was there. We use to joke that he was talking to angels. Now I know he really was. I remembered the time a few days before the plane crash when I was in my workroom and Devon was sitting on my lap. He was clearly having a little "angel conversation." Looking back, I wondered if my grandmother, knowing what was about to happen, had already begun hanging out with us.

Over the next couple of years, Devon had more "great-grandma conversations" that coincided with eventful and life-threatening experiences. One day, when Devon was about eighteen months old, I was sitting on my bed reading and could hear him having an animated conversation with someone. I jumped up to see who had come home and was surprised to see no one there. The next day was the car accident that Jessica miraculously survived.

When Devon was two and a half years old, I was working on a project in the garage. I heard him talking to someone outside as he climbed on our little John Deere tractor. I went out to see who had come over. When no one was there I asked him whom he was talking to and he answered (as if I was the dumbest mommy in the world), "Grandma!" So I said, "Oh, is Grandma Hall here?" (I thought maybe she had come by and had gone in the house.) "No! I talking to Grandma Hoen." My heart sank as I realized he meant my mother. She had been in the hospital for several weeks in poor health and wasn't expected to live much longer. I remembered in a flash that after my grandfather died, he had visited my five-year-old cousin. With my heart racing I ran inside and quickly called my mother's hospital room. When she answered the phone, the relief I felt upon hearing her familiar, beloved voice brought on the tears. I couldn't talk for a minute and knew I couldn't begin to explain my emotions to her. I simply choked out the words that I was thinking about her, loved her, and missed her.

So, whom was Devon so clearly talking to? He kept insisting it was Grandma Hoen. Later that day, I put a framed picture of my grandmother on the piano. Devon saw it, pointed, and exclaimed, "Grandma Hoen!" to which I explained to him, "No, honey. That's not Grandma

Hoen. That is Mommy's grandma, Grandma Dyer." As an afterthought I asked, "Devon, is that who you were talking to when you were playing on the tractor today?" His face brightened. "Yes! Yes! Grandma Hoen!" Through the years, as my mother had grown older, her hair had grayed and the prescriptions she was on for her rheumatoid arthritis had caused water retention, making her face rounder. I had not noticed how much she had changed and how she had come to look just like my grandmother until I studied the photo on the piano. Surely Grandma Dyer was visiting again. I put two and two together and realized that when Devon had these "conversations," life-changing events always seemed to follow.

With this realization, I became sick with worry as I took stock of what my family would be doing over the next week. Jessica was backpacking in the Grand Canyon; Jake was mountain biking in Moab; Brandon and Ryan were going waterskiing with friends at Lake Powell; Randy, Maryann, and I were going backpacking in southern Utah; and Devon was staying with a neighbor. All of us were doing potentially dangerous activities. Our guardian angel grandma was going to be way too busy.

I wanted to cancel everything and make everyone sit home where we would be safe. But then I realized I could not let fear rule our lives. I've always believed faith and fear cannot exist together, so I decided I needed to have more faith—faith that a loving Heavenly Father would watch out for all of my family members, and that the experiences we were meant to have would come our way. I prayed we would not only survive life's experiences but embrace them and learn from them. I am reminded of Psalms 46:10: "Be still, and know that I am God." It is not always easy to let God be God and know that He is truly in charge. It is hard to be grateful for problems that pull us to our knees and keep us humble. We may not be safe from grief and pain, but we are always safe in His love.

Anyway, during the next week we all went to our various adventures. I prayed for our safety and found myself talking to my grandmother as I hiked along the trail. Everyone had a great week. There were a few tense moments, like when I had to pull Maryann out of what seemed like man-devouring quicksand in a river bottom. I was beyond grateful when everyone made it through the week with only minor injuries.

The first night all of my family was back home asleep in their beds, I felt like a mother hen with her chicks tucked safely under her wing. It is a feeling only mothers and grandmothers can understand.

RANDY

The other day I was sitting in my office sending packaging designs and pictures for a new product to a design company in Phoenix, Arizona. Large graphic files sometimes take ten to fifteen minutes to send. I had a high-speed wireless Internet connection, which many people have today and which is becoming commonplace. As I was walking away from my computer I realized these pictures were being transmitted through the air, maybe right through me as I was walking around. It is almost as if the pictures were in another dimension—a dimension I can't see with my naked eyes, but yet I know is there.

Brigham Young taught that the spirit world is here among us. In my opinion, these spirits are simply in another dimension. Perhaps there are legions of angels all around us, observing our behavior, pulling for us to do the right things.

If you had lived on an island or in the Alaskan wilderness for the last twenty-five years and then came to my office and heard I was sending pictures and documents through the air with this little apparatus called a laptop, you would think I was nuts. You might say that a picture cannot be changed to invisible waves of energy and sent to places around the world for reconfiguration on a piece of paper—in color.

We exist in a world of microorganisms. With the aid of a high-powered electron microscope, we can see this world—bacteria, living cells, and the like. With a more powerful microscope such as an electron scanning microscope, we can see the molecules that make up these living cells and other chemical elements on our planet. And with an even more powerful microscope, an atomic force microscope, we can now look inside a molecule and see atomic structures or at least evidence of atoms. Within the atom are neutrons, protons, and electrons. Each chemical element has a specific number of protons and electrons. We can't see them, but atomic physicists know they are there. They also know that within protons and electrons there are subatomic particles called quarks. How do they know this? Because of the behavior of a quark. Are there particles within quarks? The answer is yes, but that is as far as we need to go.

We cannot see the contents of an atom but we can see its effects. I could not see an angel bearing my six-month-old baby in her arms, but we witnessed the effects. Our baby slammed into the metal dashboard at over one hundred miles per hour and did not receive a scratch on him. The pilot, Doug, and I were a bloody mess. The angels may have left us alone because they knew the plane was being piloted by a heavenly messenger. They knew we would live, and that the suffering would help us grow. But I believe they were there to comfort us and to direct Doug's actions, and to protect all five children on board the airplane.

I believe our world is made up of multiple dimensions. We can only see one of them. I believe there are other dimensions all around that we cannot see or hear. Someday we'll be part of this bigger picture, and we will see and understand what we cannot see or comprehend now. Until then we must walk by faith. President Spencer W. Kimball said it this way: "We need a *storage of faith* . . . Faith that can carry us over the dull, the difficult, the terrifying moments, disappointments, disillusionments, and years of adversity, want, confusion, and frustration" (Spencer W. Kimball, *Teachings of Spencer W. Kimball* [Salt Lake City: Deseret Book Co., 1982], 333; emphasis added).

EPILOGUE

HELEN

Exactly one year after the plane crash, on November 14, 1994, our family and the Wagstaff family boarded a commercial airliner and flew south for our long-awaited relaxing week in Mazatlan, Mexico. I was rather uneasy about getting on the plane and remember thinking, *Well, at least all of my family is on board. If we go down, we go down together.*

The flight was smooth until one hour before our scheduled landing time. Suddenly it was obvious the plane was losing power and descending too quickly. Beads of sweat accumulated and began running down my face. My hands started shaking while I watched flight attendants scurrying to pick up empty peanut bags and soda cups.

Thinking we were about to crash, I couldn't imagine why they were worried about a little garbage! Devon sat on my lap, and I squeezed him so tightly he started complaining.

Finally, the captain said over the intercom, "Well, folks, we've had such a strong tailwind that it looks like we will be arriving in Mazatlan about forty-five minutes early. We have begun our descent and should be landing in about ten minutes." I sighed in relief. Maybe we would live to see Mazatlan after all.

We had an enchanting week in the warm sun and relished in the charming culture of Mexico. One evening as I sat on the beach, I watched Jessica use her crutches to limp to the water's edge. Her father helped her wade through the surf into the ocean, letting the crutches drift with the waves back to the sand. Maryann and Robyn were laughing and doing cartwheels along the shore. Eighteen-month-old Devon toddled on the sand, throwing his arms up and giggling as the waves tickled his ankles. It took my breath away as I gazed at these four precious people I had nearly lost.

As the sun dropped behind the horizon, a glorious, amber-red sunset exploded in the sky and danced on the waves. I felt an indescribable, cleansing peace seep into my soul. God is in charge! No matter what trials or challenges we face in this life, He is there for us. Maybe not instantly, like He was in our plane crash, and maybe not in the way we expect, but He is always there and will help us through all things. Eventually if we allow Him in, we will feel His presence and His love every day of our lives. The peace may come quietly on a sandy beach, or forcefully during a long, lonely night, or it may feel like loving arms around us after years or even a lifetime of searching. His peace may come in different ways to different people *but it will always come.*

RANDY

People often say to us, "Going down in an airplane has to be the worst thing that could ever happen to someone!" Our response is an unequivocal, "No." The plane crash was bad in terms of the terror and physical pain we experienced, but many things in our lives have caused us more emotional pain.

Late one night after we dozed off, the phone in our bedroom rang. Our twenty-year-old daughter, Maryann, was calling from Guatemala to inform us she had been robbed at gunpoint in the jungle. My heart hurt so much for Maryann that I thought it would break.

Jacob called one evening from his apartment in Park City to tell us his neck might be broken. He had fallen while skiing off a cornice at the top of "Scott's Bowl" at Park City Ski Resort, and had slammed his head into a pine tree. At the time Jacob was a member of the ski patrol, so it went against all his training to get up, ski down the hill, and drive himself home with an injured neck. We broke speed limits driving from Midway to Park City (normally a twenty-minute drive) to rush him to the hospital. My heart just about burst with pain for my son. X-rays revealed a couple of small fractures in his neck, and he wore a brace for three months—or at least he was *supposed* to wear it for three months!

Jessica came home from Southern Utah University one day and explained that when she had broken up with her boyfriend, he had stolen her checkbook and emptied her bank account. It was not so much the money as the betrayal.

Helen already told about our trauma related to Jessica's car accident. Our children had another car accident, a rollover, while going seventy-five miles per hour in Wyoming. It was devastating for all of us. As parents, we experienced more pain than if we had been in the accident ourselves. Why is it that our children's pain can hurt us more than our own pain?

We have had many more such experiences with our children. I will not innumerate them, but I can tell you that the X-ray files at local hospitals and clinics are thick with Hall-family films.

As all parents do, we feel such indescribable pain when our children experience trauma in their lives. Usually, we can do little to help them, other than lending an empathetic ear and loving them all the more.

We watch the news and observe traumatic events in the lives of people around the world, yet some of our daily challenges and trials may run the pain meter just as high. All the more reason we have to be gentle, kind, and understanding to ourselves and to others.

There have been far too many times when we have been faced with financial difficulties and have been unable to keep our commitments. At times, our very survival seemed threatened. These times have rocked me to my very core, and caused me to question the worth of my own soul. This often brings far greater emotional trauma than the physical pain I experienced as a result of the airplane crash.

Physical pain pales when compared to our own emotional pain or feeling the pain of people we love, or even the pain of perfect strangers. This helps me understand why Jesus Christ probably suffered even more in Gethsemane than He did on the cross. The "bleeding of the pores" kind of suffering, while inconceivable to us, is an infinitely more acute suffering than bleeding from our own cuts and wounds. The Atonement required both emotional and physical suffering so we can also overcome these obstacles in our lives, overcome spiritual decline, and rise to enjoy the presence of our Savior.

This is my best answer as to whether or not the plane crash was the worst thing that ever happened to us. We are also asked how the families are doing now. The Wagstaffs are doing great. Julie had a healthy, beautiful baby boy, Jacob. He is a great little athlete with lots of blond hair. I recently watched Devon and the two youngest Wagstaff boys, Jacob and Brandon, golf together at the Homestead. These three young boys hit the ball much better than I ever did. Their blond hair stood out against the deep green grass and blue sky, and for a brief moment I could not help but have an overwhelming sense of gratitude that these three boys (who were all on the plane with us) were given a second chance to have fulfilling lives. Brittany is beautiful and sweet, and she has Julie's smile. Robyn is as beautiful inside as she is on the outside. She completed a mission for the LDS Church and is happily married.

Doug looks great. His broken back healed just fine, but he still limps slightly. His ankle, crushed in the crash, never seemed to heal completely, but that hasn't slowed him down. He and his boys run the resort at the lake in the summer, and they manage other business interests. Julie also looks wonderful with her warm and compassionate smile. Her fractured legs healed very quickly without medical attention. Her restaurant, catering business, and matriarchal duties keep her very busy. We owe such a debt of gratitude to Julie for her love, poise, and steadfastness during our ordeal. She was the rock we could all rely on. If we were asked to cross the plains like the pioneers, we would hitch our wagon right alongside Julie and Doug's. The other five children are doing well. The Wagstaffs have a wonderful family, with grandchildren coming to bring many more blessings into their lives.

What about the Halls? I think we are as crazy as ever. At my recent birthday celebration, we took a picture of all our children, our children's spouses, and our grandchildren. What a crew! There is a grand total of fifteen.

Jessica graduated from college with a degree in sociology. She and her husband Shane were directors for a wilderness youth therapy program in central Utah. They currently live in San Diego, California, with their son Aidan—our first grandson. Jessica's love and natural compassion sustain us continually.

After serving a mission in California, Jacob married a beautiful young lady who can out-climb him in the Grand Tetons. He graduated from BYU, works in industrial design, and has given us two beautiful grandchildren.

Brandon served a mission in Japan, graduated from the University of Utah in international business, and then married Kristen, the daughter of our closest friends. They have three children.

Maryann's back healed quickly, and she was back in school within weeks. She has worked in wilderness therapy as a youth counselor. She also worked with our daughter-in-law Lorien for a Norwegian outdoor exploration center, teaching young children to run rivers, rock climb, and enjoy other outdoor adventures. As stated previously, Maryann traveled to Guatemala to teach at a children's school and work in an orphanage. We love Maryann's innate spirituality and her desire to devote her life to helping children throughout the world.

Ryan served a mission to Costa Rica and is currently attending Utah Valley University. He wants a career where he can do something worthwhile and serve others, probably in the medical field.

Devon is bursting with energy and vitality, and we cannot keep up with him on the slopes or around the house. We love watching him perform in sports and grow to his potential. Some years ago on a cold night in the Arizona desert, he received a priesthood blessing where he was given a second chance to live and told he would find his purpose in life. I believe he came into this world to bless our family and to get us through the difficult times.

Helen and I are doing well. I still have some back pain, I cannot run, and I have some nerve damage, but I can go on walks and, more importantly, I can ski. I am grateful to function reasonably well and to be able to enjoy life. In fact, I was feeling so good that two years after the crash we decided to go to Grand Targhee, Wyoming, with some friends, the Steve and Jackie Hansen family, and ski the Grand Tetons again. Right before dark, near the top of the mountain, I took a jump (perhaps trying to impress my teenage kids), landed in a hole, and actually heard my leg break several times—not a pleasant sound. This was another rather painful episode, with large chunks of bone cutting through my flesh as I was hauled down from the top of the mountains in the dark and cold. An ambulance took me to the hospital in Driggs, Idaho, where they could not treat such a serious fracture, and then to Rexburg, Idaho, where they could bring in a specialist. After three surgeries, a seven-inch plate, nine screws, and several months on crutches, I walk somewhat normally.

Helen still has pain in her neck. Otherwise she is doing well, involving herself in our children's lives, the Church, the community, crafts, and enjoying her grandchildren.

We are asked if we still fly. Yes, we fly on commercial flights without fear, but we choose not to fly in small aircraft. It would be difficult if we ever found ourselves in a precarious situation again to say to the Lord, "I know you helped us before and provided a miracle, but could you do it one more time?"

When people ask if we still think about the crash, we tell them we think about it often. In fact, a day rarely goes by that we do not realize how blessed we are to be alive. We are continually grateful that we can see and talk with our kids and our other loved ones, and that we can witness firsthand the beauty of this planet and its people.

We have also come to realize something of the richness of life. It is sad that it sometimes takes a sledgehammer the size of an airplane to awaken one to this richness and beauty. At times we seem to have a heightened sense of things around us—people, the blue sky, the clouds, mountains, rivers, trees, flowers, grass, a child, a friend.

We still get frustrated with our kids on a rare occasion when they are not perfect, but we have a different perspective. We love them so much and feel so grateful to be a part of their lives on the mortality side of things that when they are not at their best, we see things in a whole different light.

The other day Helen and I were frustrated with some things, so we decided to go to our family cabin alone and pout a little, and maybe make some sense of our turmoil. First we sat out on the deck at the cabin and marveled at the greenery in the forest—the aspens, the pines, the bushes, and the plants below. We could not believe how many different shades of green the Lord has created for us. The smell of the forest was wonderfully intense. I was reminded of something Kalil Gibran said, "In the dew of little things the heart finds its morning and is refreshed."

We watched the sun shining through the trees, with beams of light highlighting certain plants. It was as if someone was moving a spotlight to show off various trees, plants, and flora. It was as if God wanted to awaken us to the beauty of His creations. One by one, our problems began to shrink and dissolve, and we felt only love. Our gratitude for being alive and being part of our children's lives far outweighed anything else. We had come so close to losing our lives, to having to watch our remaining children live out their lives from another vantage point.

I do not know all that immortality implies or what it will be like to live forever, but I do know that immortality and eternal life awaits us, *if we seek it.* I feel indebted to be here on earth at this time and to enjoy all that it has to offer. Most of all, Helen and I are profoundly grateful to be with the people we love and to enjoy this world with all its beauty.

Once again, words fall short of expressing the fullness of our emotion. We are indeed grateful for our Savior, for His Atonement, and for the divine intervention in our lives. We are thankful for the miracle of life itself—to be alive, to be loved, and to love.

Crash site near Florence, Arizona, November 14, 1993.

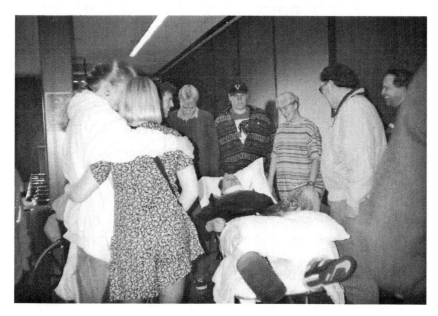

Randy arriving at Salt Lake International Airport, December 11, 1993.

Hall family, 1994. Front row, left to right: Jessica, Maryann. Back row, left to right: Randy, Helen, Devon, Brandon, Jacob, Ryan.

Hall family, 2003. Left to right: Shane (Jessica's husband), Jessica, Randy, Helen, Ryan, Brandon, Devon, Maryann, Lorien (Jacob's wife), Jacob.

Wagstaff family, 1995. Left to right: Brandon, Julie, Jacob (on shoulders), Doug, Brittany, Robyn.

Wagstaff family, 2003. © Pajun Photography

ABOUT THE AUTHORS

Helen was born in Montana and raised in Littleton, Colorado. Randy was born in Salt Lake City but grew up mostly in Southern California, where skiing, surfing, and candy making were important parts of his life. Helen and Randy graduated from Brigham Young University in 1974. They married shortly thereafter and have six children together. They started raising their children in Southern California, and then moved to Midway, Utah, where they currently reside.

Helen worked for a short time in interior design in California, but then decided to be a stay-at-home mom until the kids were mostly grown. Her real loves are her children and grandchildren, crafting, and serving in the Church, particularly in the Relief Society and Young Women organizations.

Randy was the CEO for an *Inc. 500* snack company in San Pedro, California, before moving to Utah. Randy loves skiing, fishing, hunting, boating, and playing in the mountains with his children and grandchildren. He served an LDS mission to Sweden and has served in priesthood callings and in Scouting.

Divine Intervention is Randy and Helen's first book. They would enjoy hearing from their readers and may be contacted at randy.andhelen@hotmail.com.